GEORGE
WASHING MACHINE, PORTABLES, & SUBMARINE RACES

MY ITALIAN-AMERICAN LIFE

GEORGE
WASHING MACHINE,
PORTABLES,
& SUBMARINE RACES

MY ITALIAN-AMERICAN LIFE

Story Copyright © 2019 by: Michael Cutillo
Copy Editor: Tiziano Thomas Dossena
Cover Design & Layout By: Dominic A. Campanile

ISBN: 9781691081295
Library of Congress Control Number: 2019911984

Published by: Idea Press (an imprint of Idea Graphics, LLC) — Florida (USA)
www.ideapress-usa.com • email: ideapress33@gmail.com • editoreusa@gmail.com
Printed in the USA - 1st Edition, September 2019

MICHAEL CUTILLO

GEORGE
WASHING MACHINE,
PORTABLES,
& SUBMARINE RACES

MY ITALIAN-AMERICAN LIFE

Front cover: Michael Cutillo Sr., father of the author, is shown at Westfalenstadion in Dortmund, Germany, on July 4, 2006. The stadium, with a capacity of 65,000 for international games, is the seventh largest in Europe. It was hosting a semifinal match of the 2006 FIFA World Cup men's soccer tournament between global heavyweights Italy and host Germany. The Italians defeated the Germans 2-0 in overtime in the emotionally charged game, marking the first time the German National Team had ever lost in the city of Dortmund. Italy would go on to win the world title, defeating France in the championship game played in Berlin on July 9.

PREFACE

Michael Cutillo has been a professional writer, mostly as a journalist for upstate New York newspapers, since 1982. In addition to his professional career, Michael always felt his Italian roots deep in his veins.

What better way than to combine the two – a writing career and love of his heritage – into a new adventure that began about twenty years ago when he started writing for a fraternal organization, The Order Sons of Italy in America monthly newspaper *The Golden Lion,* where his Italian culture and heritage took a welcomed leap forward as he wrote and submitted vignettes of his Italian experiences. Michael's column became an instant success, one of the "must-read" columns of the publication. Readers anxiously awaited every issue as he shared with them his love for Italy and everything Italian, and by doing so, helped many of them to relive their own experiences.

Michael was born in the United States from a love story of an Italian-American mother and Italian immigrant father. From this combination of cultures, Michael – mostly from his father – acquired an unrelenting love for Italian culture. This love brought him to Italy time after time with family and friends to experience Italy "face to face."

In this book, you will read of his many adventures in Italy with friends, especially with family he had never met before. Michael was able to communicate with them because he fluently speaks and writes in Italian. Nothing was lost in translation. Enjoy and share the beauty of his encounters in each one of the vignettes. *Buon viaggio!* to memories that may bring at least a smile to your lips and possibly a few tears to your eyes.

Sal Moschella
Editor Emeritus
Golden Lion Newspaper

Of Stories...
& Peaches

Chi va piano va sano e va lontano. – *Old Italian proverb*

Literally: He who goes slowly, goes safely and goes far.

English equivalent: Slow and steady wins the race.

I collect stories.

I know many people who collect any number of other items — usually much more tangible — stamps, maybe; leather-bound books about World War II; fancy wines; porcelain figurines. All nice. But I enjoy sitting around listening to tales, real-life tales. It could be in the middle of the winter, with a toasty fire crackling in the fireplace and a rich cup of coffee at hand, maybe spiked with a few drops of anisette. Or it could be in the heat of the summer at a backyard picnic table, a soft warm breeze in the air with a nice glass of homemade red wine filled with chopped up peaches nearby.

If that last sentence resonates with you, we could be kindred souls … or *paisani.*

It's tradition in my Dad's family to load up the *vino* in the summertime with fresh fruit, usually juicy peaches — though the fruit also could be cherries, grapes, raspberries, even lemons or oranges. The idea is to cut up that fruit into bite-size chunks, put them in whatever you are using for a decanter and then fill and refill that decanter however many times over the course of your storytelling session. It's not exactly sangria, but it's similar. A few pieces of the fruit may plop into your drinking glass, and that's OK. Better than OK, really. But most of them will remain in the decanter, soaking up the wine until the sipping and the tales are finished. Then you take out the fruit – the grapes or peaches or whatever – that has been marinating in that wine for the entire time and you munch on a delectable, wine-soaked treat. My first recollection of wine as a youngster, in fact, is not a glass of it but rather a peach slice that had been soaked in it.

That's a big part of the whole experience in my Italian-American family.

The other part, of course, are those stories themselves, usually coming from Dad, also named Michael Cutillo, *Michele* in Italian – pronounced not like our female name Michelle but rather "me-KAY-lay." He is 88 years young as I write this in 2019 but remembers the olden, sepia-toned and black-and-white days as if they were yesterday. Stories about meeting our Mom, an 18-year-old American girl, in his village in 1955; trying to follow her to America but being unsuccessful because he didn't know the emigration laws; then finally managing to make his way to the States only to realize that he could speak but a few words of English. Honestly, there's only so deep you can go in a conversation with a vocabulary that consists entirely of "Hello, Joe" (which is how they greeted the U.S. soldiers, or GI Joes, who were stationed in his village during World War II) and "cigarettes" (which is what they used to barter with those soldiers for things like soccer balls and shoes).

You'll meet my Dad and you'll read many of those anecdotes — and more — as you leisurely make your way through this book, this collection of tales that stretches from the Old Country where my family originated, to America where Mom and Dad raised me and my three sisters, and then back to the Old Country to see it through my own eyes and my own experiences, especially as I have led a number of group trips to *bell'Italia*. They are the stories that I have culled over the years. Many are time-worn and have been told and retold in my family so often most of us can recite them while we are *dormendo* – that is, sleeping. You'll read about George Washing Machine and my shiny new "portable," "choir practice" and how dad chops the ending off English words so that "corner" becomes "corn" and "pocket" is "pock."

You may have some relatives who do the same thing, and that is part of my goal in presenting this personal collection. It's not meant to be only about me, but rather I hope the stories strike a chord, that they remind you of your own families, whether you are of Italian lineage or not. You could be Spanish or French, Russian or Mexican, Chinese or African and had family members – or even yourself – who fumbled their way at first in these wonderful United States. After all, America is not only the greatest immigrant nation on the face of the Earth, but it is precisely those immigrants who built it into the greatest nation – period – in the history of the world.

One of Dad's endearing qualities is that even as he stumbled over the language and botched his driver's test five times, he never let it get him down, he just kept plugging away, especially with a young family on the way – I was born in 1960 followed at fairly regular intervals by my three sisters. *Michele*, whose grandfather also was named *Michele* – imagine that! – was born in the small southern Italian village of San Salvatore Telesino in 1931. Chances are you've never heard of it. He lived there, picking grapes, eating chestnuts and kicking soccer balls, until his great adventure in America began in 1958. But he was unlike so many other thousands of Italian immigrants who couldn't get out of Italy fast enough, fleeing their homeland because of the poverty and the lack of work. Dad and his farming family weren't rich, but they were content. He loved Italy and in fact, had just gained acceptance to the police academy when he met Mom and decided to follow a different path, a path that he had never imagined in his wildest dreams. So, he left to start a new life and his own family 4,000 miles away, but he never turned his back on Italy, as so many immigrants who came to America did, folks who, once they began chasing the American Dream, never had any desire to return to their poor, downtrodden homeland to chase something they knew they could not catch. Dad went back often, over fifty times. I've always said that he gave us the best of two worlds because he loved Italy dearly and he learned to love the United States even more.

I've heard him tell people numerous times, "I live in the greatest country in the world … and I was born in the second greatest country in the world."

Then he would launch into one of those stories of his … and sip that wine with the peaches.

Speaking of peaches, I always use them as a metaphor to highlight Dad's special, optimistic, glass-is-more-than-half-full outlook on life. Even at 88 years of age, if a man offered him two peach pits and said, "If you plant these pits today, in 20 years you will have the most unbelievable, the juiciest, the tastiest peaches you have ever experienced in your life," my Dad would accept them and plant them.

His reasoning would be threefold: OK, the man said it would take 20 years to produce those incredible peaches, but hey, you never know, maybe – if the conditions are just right – they'll be ready in a year or two. That's the optimist in him. Secondly, Dad would be thinking, "Let's see, 20 years from now I would be 108; yep, chances are I'll still be around." And thirdly, if those two peach trees don't reach full maturity until all those 20 years, and Dad has rejoined Mom in heaven by then, he figures at least his family and friends will get to enjoy the most amazing peaches ever. That's how much he cares about us and all those around him.

In my 35 years as a journalist in upstate New York, I've written about many of the stories in this book in one form or another. Some of the essays were previously published in newspapers or in "The Golden Lion," the monthly newsletter of the state Order Sons and Daughters of Italy in America for which I am a regular contributor. Others are a compilation of a couple of essays, while still others are entirely new, written solely for this effort and added to the collection.

It also is often said that the Italian language with all its dialects is rich with compelling and provocative proverbs and that there is a saying for almost everything – some humorous, some sage, some even confusing – so I also have begun each chapter, including this Introduction, with an Italian phrase or proverb that relates to the chapter.

So, it is part memoir and autobiographical and part biographical about my Dad *Michele* and our family. It is a journal, a little bit of a history book and part travelogue. It doesn't contain recipes, but we'll talk about food and drink like a cookbook. It contains language lessons, and we have even thrown in some photographs. It's a lot of things rolled into one, sort of like any collection ought to be.

With all of that, I invite you to sit back, relax, chop up those peaches. And above all enjoy.

Andiamo! Let's go!

TABLE OF CONTENTS

LA
FAMIGLIA

THE
FAMILY

The first time my Mom and Dad met, in the summer of 1955, they would take walks in the hills near San Salvatore Telesino, usually with the family in tow a respectful distance behind, and sometimes climbing up a few rocks as in this shot.

My Mom and Dad ended up having three very happy and festive wedding ceremonies, including this first one in San Salvatore Telesino in 1957 that made their union legal. Once they were married, Dad was able to come to the United States with no immigration issues.

1

Una Storia D'Amore (A Love Story)

Chi ha quattrini conta, chi ha bella moglie canta. – *Italian proverb*

Literally: Those who have money spend their time counting; those who have a beautiful wife, sing.

Every family story must first begin with a love story.

Ours begins in the summer of 1955. Pasqualina Sylvia Tucci was 18 years old, just out of high school in a small upstate New York village near Syracuse called Warners. She was trying to figure out what she was going to do with the rest of her life. She was sharp, had an aptitude for numbers and had worked some odd jobs, but her main responsibilities at the time were helping her Mom on the family farm and looking after her four younger siblings. They were the same things she'd basically been doing since she was six and their father Dominick died at the shockingly young age of 43.

That summer of '55, she would make a special trip with her Grandmother Pasqualina to her *nonna's* hometown, San Salvatore Telesino, in the southern Italian province of Benevento. It was going to be something of a working vacation because her *nonna* could not read English, especially the labeling on the pill bottles that contained her daily medications. Commonly known by her middle name, Sylvia was the one who was going to make sure that *nonna* took those meds properly and precisely.

Fate played a bit of a role in this – doesn't it always in so many love stories? – because Sylvia actually was the second choice to travel with *nonna*. Her Uncle Rudy, *Zio Rudolfo*, had been selected as *nonna's* caretaker, but he mussed up those plans when he decided to get married that

In 1955, when Mom and Dad first met, they sometimes walked to the neighboring town of Telese where there was a movie theater. There was a field on the way with a stream gently passing through it, and Dad would place a watermelon in the stream so that when they returned on their way home, it would be chilled by the cool mountain waters. This is a shot of Mom and Dad in that field in San Salvatore Telesino.

spring. A new husband could not leave his bride for an entire summer, especially the first summer of their married life.

Michele Cutillo, meanwhile, was 24 that summer. He, too, was not quite sure where life was going to take him or what he wanted to do with it. School wasn't for him, that was for certain, and he left it after the fourth grade to help his parents on their farm in San Salvatore Telesino. His passion was sport, especially soccer, and he was happiest when he had a ball at his feet. However, that was impractical, his *mamma* had determined – "The ball won't feed you," she used to say. So, Michele worked the farm and vineyards while dreaming of other pursuits. Recently, he had been accepted into the local police academy, which had taken some pulling of strings because Michele was just under the height requirement. It wasn't his dream job, becoming a member of the *carabinieri*, but at least as a cop, he would be out of those fields, and he would make a good, solid living.

Sylvia and Michele definitely were traveling different paths, but in the summer of 1955, those paths converged.

Because Michele's village was the same one Sylvia's *nonna* was from, the two youngsters met through mutual friends and family members and quickly became fast friends. It didn't hurt, by a long stretch, that Michele's family's house in the village had a bathroom and running water, while the farm house of Sylvia's *nonna's* family out in the country did not. When Sylvia, the teen-aged American girl, learned this, she asked if she could possibly use the Cutillo bathroom to do the primping that all teen girls, from any country, need to do. Michele's parents said yes, surely.

Michele and Sylvia could not really speak much to each other. Save for a few words, Michele spoke no English, and Sylvia spoke little Italian other than some dialect. Yet, through a combination of those few words, a few gestures and some eye contact, they were able to communicate and enjoy each other's company all summer. They often took long, slow walks – usually with family members in tow, a respectful distance away – climbing the numerous hills around San Salvatore Telesino, picking fresh fruit off the abundant trees and gazing into each other's eyes. One thing they enjoyed doing was walking to the movie theater in the nearby town of Telese. It was only about five kilometers, around three miles, and on the way, Michele would place a fresh, juicy watermelon in the crystal-clear mountain stream that ran between the two villages. On their way back after the show, they would stop at the melon, now quite chilled, and sit in the field next to the stream, enjoying the juicy fruit and each other's company.

Later in the summer, it was determined that Castelvenere would be a better town for Sylvia's *nonna* to live in. It was just a few kilometers east of Telese and a little higher elevation than San Salvatore Telesino. Pasqualina had suffered a heart attack earlier in 1955, back in the States, and the feeling was that the fresher air in Castelvenere would be better for her, so they went to stay with a relative there. Michele had no automobile so he would pedal his bicycle the five or so miles to visit Sylvia in Castelvenere whenever he could. They went to parties together, even to a wedding. Sylvia had a boyfriend named Bob in America, and when she showed Michele Bob's picture, he ripped it up and said, *"Tu sei mia."* You are mine!

Alas, the summer came to an end, but when it did, Sylvia and Michele vowed to remain in contact. They wrote each other frequently, especially Sylvia, who sometimes wrote and sent two or three letters a day. Michele wrote in Italian, and Sylvia would have the letters translated into English. She would write back in English, and he had them translated into Italian. Some may say that was no way to have a courtship, but those two? Well, they fell more and more in love through those translated letters, so much so that they eventually decided to get married.

Sylvia asked Michele to come to America for the wedding, and he agreed, dropping out of the police academy, to his father's chagrin. However, being naïve about the process of leaving Italy for America – and never having explored it before – he failed. Twice.

The first time, after a large, festive going-away party in San Salvatore Telesino for family and friends, Michele took the train to Naples with a few possessions and all the money he had in the world, about $200. He was intent on boarding a ship to America, and he knew that they departed from Naples frequently. In the big city, which had a reputation for being somewhat shady, he was wandering the streets near the port and all those ships when a man on a street corner asked him what he was looking for. Michele told him he wanted to get to America. The man asked how much money he had. When Michele told him $200, the man proclaimed, "This is your lucky day, son, because that is exactly how much it costs to go to America. If you give it to me, I will help you get there." Excitedly, Michele handed the man all the money he had in the world … and the man ran off with it!

Broke and broken-hearted, Michele took a train back to San Salvatore Telesino, much to the surprise of his parents and friends. He was determined now more than ever to research the proper procedures that would allow him to set sail for America. He learned that he needed to have an interview at the Consulate in Naples and that the interviewer would determine if he could emigrate. There were a number of acceptable reasons to go to America, including jobs and family members that were waiting on the other side of the Atlantic. One quite unacceptable reason was to go there simply to marry an American girl. The interview was going well, or so Michele thought. He told the interviewer, a woman, that he was going to meet uncles in Pennsylvania – brothers of his mother Teresa – and that they had a job lined up for him. He thought he was doing beautifully until the interviewer abruptly stamped his application DENIED! Stunned by the rejection, he asked why. "Because," the examiner said tersely, "I know you are going over there to marry an American girl." His eyes gave him away she told him.

Rejected and dejected a second time, Michele caught yet another train back to his village, again surprising his parents upon yet another return. He wrote to Sylvia another of those letters only this time he told her, sadly, that he didn't think he would ever get to America. She wrote back, having done a bit of homework herself, and suggested that if she returned to Italy and married him, legally he would then be free, with an American wife, to go to the United States. That became the new plan. Sylvia returned to Italy – the second and actually only other time she would ever go there – and she and Michele were married late in 1957 in San Salvatore Telesino's pretty little Church of Santa Maria Assunta. In May of 1958, Michele flew – forget those ships! – with his bride to New York City and from there, they headed north to Syracuse where they would start their new life together.

Interestingly, the young couple actually would have three beautiful and festive wedding celebrations – that first one in San Salvatore Telesino with Michele's relatives, the second in Sylvia's tiny upstate village of Warners with her relatives, and a third in Pennsylvania with Michele's cousins who had put their roots down in the Jeannette area east of Pittsburgh.

Michele – Michael in English – and Sylvia went on to have a long and fruitful life, raising four successful American children – Michael, Teresa, Lisa and Jennifer – and granddaughters Kristine and Lexi all while keeping alive the traditions of the homeland.

Sound like a Hollywood story? Well, this tale does not come from the fanciful imagination of some screenwriter. It's all true. It's the story of my Mom and Dad. They would have celebrated the 50th anniversary of their "American" wedding in September of 2008, but Mom died that February. In 2019, Dad is still with us.

And he is still telling us the story of Michele and Sylvia … and all those love letters.

Dad stands next to a Chevy Impala. I'm not sure if it's exactly the car that he used for his driving test when all four doors flew open – turn around and go home! – but it very well could be. (See Chapter 2)

2

Of George Washing Machine & Submarine Races

La vita è una battaglia. Chi non lotta, diventa presto un uomo di ricotta.
– Italian proverb on fate and fortune

Literally: Life is a battle. Those who cannot fight have to quickly become men made of ricotta. (In other words, you have to figure things out).

When I was younger – and yes, quite uninformed – I would whine to my Dad about not teaching me Italian when I was an infant, an age when it is supposed to be easiest to learn any language.

Eventually, I would take Italian classes at St. John Fisher College in Rochester, New York, and learn the language well enough. I almost had enough credits to minor in it. It was during that time, while reviewing some lessons at home with Dad over one break, that he told me the reason he hadn't taught me earlier: When I was born in 1960, it was more important for him to learn English; much more important. He needed to find work, which he couldn't do if he couldn't speak. It wasn't that he didn't want to teach me his native tongue, but reality spoke a bit louder than his desires.

When Dad came to the United States in 1958 after marrying Mom, he knew exactly three words of English – "Hello, Joe" and "cigarettes" – so unless you happened to be named Joe or you wanted a smoke, Dad didn't really have much to offer, conversation-wise.

An aside: "Hello, Joe" became a bit of a calling card in our family. Even my grandfather – who also spoke absolutely no English – used the phrase. When I visited him with Dad in 1974, every morning, grandpa would greet me with "Hello, Joe" and a smile. Later, when *nonno* came to America on one of his two trips here, my sister Lisa had a boyfriend who actually was named Joe, and when she introduced him to *nonno*, and he said, "Hello, Joe," Joe turned to Lisa and said, "How does he know my name?"

Back to Dad in his early days in the United States. With a young family quickly on the way, it was vital for him to learn the new language and not quite so vital to teach his infant son the old one. It worked. Dad learned English relatively rapidly – mostly by watching television, believe it or not.

However, there were a few bumps in the road.

He had to take his driver's test five times, not because he was a reckless driver but because he couldn't understand what the examiner was asking. Also, in those days, the first portion of the exam was given orally in the car; if you passed that, you continued on with the driving portion. Dad failed the oral exam twice and says the examiner would punctuate his failure by reciting a phrase that Dad also learned quickly via repetition: "Turn around and go home."

The third time, he thought up a scheme that involved his mother-in-law and a piece of string. Family members were allowed to be in the vehicle in the backseat during the exam, so Dad proposed tying a long, thin string to one of his fingers and to one of his mother-in-law's, and when Grandma Josie heard the question, she was supposed to tug on that string one time if the answer was A, twice if it was B and three times if it was C. They practiced it at home before going to the examination. Perfect, right? Wrong. Grandma Josie decided at the last minute that she just could not go through with the devious game plan, and she declined to tug on the string.

Left to his own devices, Dad failed. Again. Turn around and go home. Again.

When he finally did pass the first portion it was primarily because the rules had been modified, and it was no longer an oral first portion but a written one that was conducted in an office. Pass that, and then go drive. Another young man was taking the written test at the same time, and Dad isn't ashamed to say – in fact, he says so proudly – that he peeked over his shoulder at the other guy's answers and basically copied them. He was quick witted about the whole thing, too, though, because he figured he shouldn't have all his answers exactly the same as the other fellow's. That wouldn't look right. So, he changed a few Bs to As, a few Cs to Bs, and he passed. Truth is, he earned a better score than the other man!

So, the star pupil, feeling full of himself, finally moved on to the driving portion. He still couldn't understand verbal instructions very well, but he definitely understood that the examiner wanted him to drive through a particular intersection up ahead. Dad was tooling along nicely when he got into the middle of that intersection and noticed the back of a stop sign, ahead on the other side of the intersection. With terrific peripheral vision, he also noted stops signs on the left corner and on the right corner, and he correctly came to the conclusion that "This must be a four-way stop intersection and there must be a stop sign behind me that I just drove past." So, in the center of that intersection, he did what anyone would have done once the realization struck like a lightning bolt: He slammed on the brakes. He was driving his mother-in-law's rickety old Chevy, as he tells it, and when he abruptly laid on those brakes, all four doors of that car flew open! The examiner lurched forward and almost struck his head on the dashboard.

When he collected himself, smoothed out his messed-up hair, well ... you can guess what he said: Turn around ... and go home!

Despite all the trials and tribulations, Dad eventually earned his American driver's license, but it sure took some doing.

He also tells the joke on himself about the time when he was attending classes ahead of taking his test to become a U.S. citizen. The teacher had lectured for a while about American history and customs and then was asking the class a few questions. When he asked who the first president of the United States was, Dad, with great enthusiasm, quickly shot up his arm, knowing for sure that he had the answer. When called upon, Dad proudly and confidently answered, in his very best broken English, "George ... Washing Machine!"

Dad said the class erupted in laughter, though we never really knew if that story was true or not because he always tells it with a mischievous twinkle in his eye. It did show us, however, that it surely helped to have a sense of humor while learning a new language, along with the ability to laugh at yourself.

I never had a problem understanding Dad and his broken English, and growing up, I just assumed everyone else could understand him perfectly well, too.

The first time my dad gave a girlfriend and me a ride to our high school for homecoming ceremonies, she sat in the front seat with Dad, and they had a nice conversation all the way to the football field. I thought to myself, "Wow, this is terrific that my girlfriend is getting along so well with Dad."

After he dropped us off and we said goodbye, she turned to me and said, "You know, I couldn't understand one word he said."

He also had an interesting way of pronouncing those English words, once he learned them. I think it has a lot to do with his native language, which is influenced by dialects, the ending of a word – sometimes, in fact, the *entire* word – being different in one village down south than in another village up north, for example.

In keeping with what is familiar, then, Dad also chops off the endings of a lot of English words. Pocket, for example, becomes pock, as in, "Pick up that stone and put it in your *pock*." Mountain becomes mount: "We'll go pick up the cheese in that little village up the *mount*." Corner becomes corn: "It's near that little shop on the *corn*." Even a holiday like Easter becomes East: "Hey, everybody, happy *East!*"

More complex words, naturally, are infinitely more troubling. A road in my hometown of Baldwinsville was named for our eighth president, Martin Van Buren. Dad called it, as best as I could tell, "Van Beer Road." I honestly can't say how he came by that pronunciation, but that's what it was. He also worked in a machine shop on a Syracuse city street named for a pre-Colonial Native American leader of the Onondaga and the Mohawk, Hiawatha. Being that "h's" are silent in Italian and that the "th" combination becomes a hard T sound, Dad pronounced it "Iawatt."

These were names of streets I had heard all my life growing up, so imagine my own problems when I began driving and had to ask directions to get to Van Beer Road or to Iawatt Boulevard!

Also, as much as words and grammar were one thing, sometimes those dastardly slang phrases threw him off, understandably so I would say. One time, he was driving a bunch of my friends and me home from a baseball game when we passed Onondaga Lake, a small lake that was renowned in the Syracuse area as sort of a hangout spot for young lovers.

True to form, as we drove by on the star-lit, romantic, summer night, numerous cars were parked along the boulevard with their occupants undoubtedly gazing at those stars and enjoying some *amore.*

One of us, using a well-worn phrase of the day about such activities, said, "Gee, must be they're watching the submarine races tonight."

We teens in the car giggled nervously at the titillating suggestion, while Dad just drove on without saying anything. I could tell, though, that he was processing that one and trying to figure it out. Finally, he could contain himself no longer.

"How in the hell," he asked, quite earnestly, "do they get submarines in that lake?"

We all broke up.

Before he landed his job as a welder and metal worker, he tried a number of other occupations, including hairdresser. My Uncle Louie owned a beauty shop, and dad took classes to get his hairdressing license. Styling hair, though, drove him crazy because he says sometimes, he would do what he considered to be a magnificent, lovely job on a woman's hairdo and the customer would despise it. At other times, he was frightened himself when he finished up a 'do and was terrified that the customer was going to loathe it, and she would turn to him and say it was the prettiest cut she'd ever had.

So, he didn't last long in that career, though he insists that the customers really adored him. I asked how he knew that, and he told me,

"Oh, easy, because they used to call me The Butcher." Or more precisely, in Dad's chop-it-up dialect, he said, "The Butch."

Now, being a butcher back in Italy – or a *macellaio* – is, indeed, quite an honorable and sought-after profession, which is why Dad thought the women were fawning over him when they laid that nickname on him. I had to break the news to him that in English, it is not … exactly… such… a… good… thing to be known as a butcher in a beauty shop.

On the other hand, having an Italian-speaking father did come in handy on more than a few occasions and led to some interesting scenarios.

When I was a junior in high school, our varsity soccer team was playing a playoff tournament match against a Syracuse city school. We were a good team from Baldwinsville, but we played in a county (read: rural) league and were taking on a private city school, Henninger, that was undefeated and loaded with international (read: mostly Italian) superstar players.

Dad sat in the stands with my aunt on the cold, nippy, dark fall night. Behind him sat two men, bundled up tightly in black overcoats against the chill, fedoras pulled down low. They were speaking Italian, loud enough for anyone around them to hear but not thinking there was anyone who could understand what they were saying.

"We ought to kill this team tonight," they said. "They play out in the country, out in Baldwinsville, like a bunch of donkeys, a bunch of mules. They are farmers. They can't play like us."

They continued on like that for most of the game, but lo and behold, about halfway through, we scored a goal to take a 1-0 lead.

"Ah, that's not a problem, not a problem at all against this team of B'ville donkeys. They'll fold like the farmers they are in a little bit. They are really just mules."

As my aunt who was sitting with Dad tells it, she had to squeeze his hand to keep him from turning around and confronting the men. So he bit his tongue … until, about 10 minutes later, I scored a second goal and we were ahead 2-0!!

Well, that was that. Dad could not contain his excitement any longer. He turned around to face the two Italian men and, shaking both fists triumphantly, started braying like a donkey.

"Ee-awwwwww, ee-awwwwww, ee-awwwwww!!!"

The men – talk about being caught with your hand in the donkey jar! – were quiet the rest of the night as we walked off the field with a 2-0 upset win.

Dad also has coined more than a few phrases in his 60 years in America, usually some sort of combination of broken English and Italian. He probably is most renowned for "whose care," a mispronunciation – or let's say special pronunciation – of "who cares" that is favored by friends and family members alike.

It's used like this:

"Hey Dad, there's no more macaroni."

"Ah, whose care."

To piggyback off that, our friend Mary once asked Dad how he would say "whose care" in Italian. Trying to be funny instead of purely literal, he came up with *Chi se ne frega* for her, which actually is a bit profane, translated more precisely as "Who gives a damn." (And as a gimmick to remember that phrase, Mary uses, to all of our amusement, "Keys in the Vega).

Another phrase is "Sciué sciué." Dad didn't coin it – it is from the Neapolitan dialect, pronounced "shoo-WAY, shoo-WAY," and it basically means "quick quick" or "fast fast" – but he introduced it to all his friends and relatives in America.

The phrase is used primarily in referring to cooking, and I have even seen interviews by perhaps the most famous Neapolitan, actress Sophia Loren, saying she's not necessarily a great cook, but she's good at putting together a "sciué sciué" meal.

That's how Dad introduced it to me. I could be out late with friends when some hunger pangs would strike us. I'd call him and ask if I could bring the guys over for a quick bite, and he'd say, "Sure, give me 15 minutes and I'll put together something sciué sciué."

By the time we'd arrive, 15 minutes later, sure enough there would be a quick marinara sauce steaming on the stove and macaroni cooked and ready to soak up that sauce. A few slices of bread, a glass of vino, and there's your sciué sciué meal.

These days, many of us have taken to using the phrase in unconventional ways. My wife, if she just needs to take a quick shower to rinse off, will say she's taking a "sciué sciué shower"; a friend, when he needs to do a quick fix-up job on a living room shelf will call it a "sciué sciué fix"; another friend might say he can't come over for a glass of wine until he mows his lawn sciué sciué.

You get the point, and hey, if it's good enough for Sophia Loren, it's got to be good enough for our crowd, right?

When I think about all these stories – and all my friends who are using words and phrases originated by Dad – I just have to laugh and think that a guy who knew only a handful of words when he first came to America has now, in a way, birthed his very own language that people far and wide are using.

He's gotten pretty good with the rascally English language, too, or at least he would like you to think so. When he goes back to the Old Country and sits around with all his relatives who also speak only a few words of English, he is the undisputed English professor, which I laugh about and think to myself, "That's kind of scary."

Primarily because even these days, some things throw him off.

Not too long ago, I pulled into his driveway with my brand new, shiny Mustang convertible.

"Hey, Dad, check out my new car," I gushed.

His eyes lit up with pride when he saw it.

"Holy cow," he exclaimed. "A portable!"

3

Red Tape,
Italian Style

(Editor's note: This story first ran in the Finger Lakes Times newspaper in 2000.)

Chi vuoi vivere e star bene – prende il mondo come viene. – *Italian proverb*

Literally: Who wants to live and keep well – takes the world as it comes. (Basically, live and let live. Or another way to look at it, don't worry, be happy.)

For a guy who doesn't exist, my father makes a pretty good meatball.

Rolls a mean bocce ball, too.

Seriously, my Dad does exist – I mean, I don't think I would be sitting here at this keyboard if he didn't. But the problem is that for the past few months, he has been trying to get the officials in his hometown of San Salvatore Telesino to believe that he's around.

Here's the story, and if it sounds like a bad Joe Pesci movie, I apologize:

It starts back in 1998 when officials in Dad's small farming village in the province of Benevento began going through records, attempting to identify all the village's property owners. Why they picked then for a village that's been around for over 5,000 years – *chi sa?* Who knows. New tax regulations or something.

Dad, who moved to the United States in 1958 after marrying Mom, still owns an apartment on Via Roma. It's near Salvatore's butcher shop, around the corner from a café owned by his *cugino* Luigi and right next door to his *cumpare* Anselmo. But I digress.

Because Dad lives in America now, he doesn't have to pay taxes on that property, which is the good news. The bad news is that all records of Dad emigrating from San Salvatore Telesino to the United States of America had either been lost, misplaced, stolen or tossed into the barrel when they made wine last fall; makes for a nice blend when mixed with *trebbiano* grapes.

OK, so village officials contacted my uncle, who also owns property in the village and in the nearby city of Caserta. My *Zio Enzo*, a retired general in the Italian army, was adamant that his brother existed. The general's good word, however, was not good enough.

So, Zio Enzo called Dad and told him that those village officials wanted a list of Italian consulates and embassies in the eastern portion of the United States and that they would then do the remainder of the work in verifying Dad's existence. My father called me and asked me to find the addresses of those consulates and embassies, which I was able to do easily enough on the internet. We sent them off to the good folks in the San Salvatore Telesino municipal office.

A few months later, Dad gets word that records for a Michele (Michael) Cutillo have been located, birth date of February 12, 1935.

Terrific.

Except Dad was born May 8, 1931.

Next, he gets a call from the nearest vice consul, who is located in Rochester, New York. She advises him that he needs to get to Rochester for an interview. Dad, who lives in Syracuse, about 90 minutes away, tells her that this is inconvenient because he doesn't drive, and he asks if they can do the interview over the phone.

Dad really does drive, but this is known in the existence-verifying business as a little white lie.

She's not buying. "Get a ride," she tells him.

That's where I come in. Just call me chauffeur.

The consulate's address is 185 Empire Boulevard, and as we cruise into the city of Rochester, we're on the lookout for a stately building with imposing iron gates and guards posted out front. What we get, however, is a residential neighborhood and Empire Travel, a travel agency in a converted house at 185 Empire.

In the window sits a small blue plastic sign, about the size of one your grocery store uses to announce its special on *capicola*, that reads "Consulate." Inside, mixed in amid travel posters for Venice and sunny Italy, are three desks along one wall – two belong to travel agents who work there and the one in the middle belongs to the Vice Consul, a Mrs. Agada. A very pleasant woman, as it turns out.

Dad has his interview – where have you lived, how many children, where have you worked over the years, etc. He shows her his passport and shakes her hand.

Elapsed time: Eight minutes. Maybe.

The months-long adventure seemed all but over, but Dad was still shaking his head as we exited the travel agency ... er, consulate. To reassure him, I said, "Hey, look at the bright side, Dad ... at least you exist now."

"*Aspetta*," he said. "Wait. Not so fast. I still don't exist until those papers get to the Old Country. And we know how the mail works over there!"

4

Mamma, The Lifeblood of the Family and Now Our Guardian Angel

Il più bel dono di Dio è il cuore della mamma. – *Italian proverb*

Literally: God's most beautiful gift is a mother's heart.

My mom's favorite holiday was Easter. She was one of the most devout Catholics I've ever known, and I'm certain that's an important factor in why it meant something special to her. I didn't realize until later in life, though, that it probably also had something to do with her very name.

Mom, you could say, was all but named after the Christian holiday that celebrates Jesus' resurrection.

While she generally went by Sylvia, which was her middle name, her first name – rarely heard around our household – was Pauline. Many of you probably realize that Pauline was an anglicized version of her true, given first name, the Italian *Pasqualina*. She was named after her grandmother.

Pasqua is the Italian word for Easter. Mom's name literally means "Child of Easter."

If you don't know any Pasqualinas, that's not a surprise. It's the feminine version of Pasquale – one of the top 20 names in Italy but not nearly as fashionable in America. Apparently, it reached its peak popularity in 1911 when 36 babies per million were named Pasqualina. The website babycenter.com proclaimed that in 2015, it was the 15,354th most popular baby name, though I suppose if you're 15,354th in something, you're really not *all* that popular. Which is the point.

Another quick Google search landed a website which noted that from 1880 until 2013, only 627 baby girls in America were given the moniker Pasqualina. Think about that for a second: In a 133-year period, just over 600 babies were bestowed with that name, an average of about five per year. Generally, in recent years, about 4 million babies are born in the United States annually, which means that a staggeringly small .000125 percent of them are conferred with that beautiful name of Pasqualina.

In 1937, my Mom, born in the United States of Italian-American parents, was one of the .000125 percent.

All that is to say that Easters were truly special in our family. Mom celebrated 70 of them before she died in 2008, about one month before what would have been her 71st *Pasqua*, and we've missed her ever since. Whoever said time eases all sadness … well, I think that person hasn't lost his or her *mamma*. I still think about mine every day.

Neither Mom nor Dad steered any of their four children toward specific careers, but Mom is clearly the reason I have been involved with the written word for a career that is closing in on the 40-year mark. She was a voracious reader and even did a little writing herself, though not for publications, simply because she liked to.

I remember in 2006 when Dan Brown's novel "The DaVinci Code" was the red-hot read. My girlfriend bought the book for her daughter as a Christmas gift, and after shopping that day in Syracuse, New York, we stopped at Mom and Dad's house for dinner. Jan told Mom about the book, and Mom said she was something like 357th on a waiting list at the local library to read it. Even though it was going to be a gift, Jan very graciously told Mom she could borrow the one she just bought for her daughter if she wanted to. Mom's eyes lit up. She promised that she wouldn't bend the pages or crease the spine and would return it, just like new, as quickly as possible. We really weren't concerned about that; we just wanted Mom to get a chance to read it.

The next evening, we were at a function at our local Sons of Italy Lodge in Geneva, New York. My buddy Pete Pashley had stopped at Mom and Dad's house earlier that afternoon and said he had something for us from Mom. He handed us Jan's copy of "The DaVinci Code." Mom had finished it ... in one night!

And no, there were no creases or smudges on it.

I mean, are you kidding me? Have you read that book? It's a complicated, somewhat controversial story that took me about a month to read and digest. Mom polished it off in one night, loved it, remembered absolutely every last detail in the complex tale and discussed it almost reverently with anyone who brought it up.

That is my definition of a voracious reader. And of my Mom.

Christmas also was a well-loved holiday for Pasqualina Sylvia Tucci Cutillo, and because of that, everyday is Christmas at our house – literally. Or at least, every time I walk into our kitchen, I think of the Yuletide season, thanks to Mom.

Unlike many Christmas decorations that get pulled out of the attic and dusted off sometime around Thanksgiving, we have a colorful ceramic Christmas tree that resides on the kitchen counter all year long. It's about eight inches tall and sort of presides over the other knick-knacks from a prominent spot next to the toaster oven. It lights up with the flick of a small switch, thanks to a one of those old-fashioned pointy bulbs that used to serve as real Christmas tree bulbs. The small white bulb is screwed into a socket in the base, and when it is on, its white light illuminates different-colored plastic pegs that serve as the "bulbs" for the ceramic tree. The yellow star on top broke off years ago, but otherwise it's in perfect shape.

We often keep it on all night — in all its Christmassy, multi-colored glory — to serve as our kitchen nightlight. To be honest, there have been times when I haven't remembered switching it on before we went to bed, found it illuminated in the morning, and asked my wife, "Hey, did you turn the Christmas tree light on?" And she'll say, "No, I didn't."

Cue the Twilight Zone music.

Of course, I probably had turned it on, but I prefer to think that maybe Mom had something to do with it.

Mom — in addition to raising four kids, working a number of different jobs, keeping her boisterous Italian husband in line, and being the matriarch for her own brothers and sister who lost their mother and father early — had a number of hobbies over the years; usually in spurts. She loved quilting for a while ... and sewing ... and putting puzzles together. And, for a short period of time, she was into ceramics. *Really* into ceramics.

Family members became the recipients of any number of Mom's ceramic handiwork. I was probably about 20 when she made me a beautiful set of chess pieces. I really loved them and all, but there was one thing: What does a 20-year-old, who is moving from dorm room to dorm room, then apartment to apartment, do with a set of ceramic chess pieces?

I kept them stored securely over the years in the white JCPenney box that she used to gift them to me — carting them from apartment closet to basement to attic — until just a couple of years ago when our friends Pete and Diane gave us a shiny, wooden chessboard that Diane's pop Tony had made. It is in our dining room with those chess pieces adorning it; no one plays it because I'm afraid those dainty ceramic pieces will get broken, but it's a great decoration and conversation piece.

The Christmas tree was another ceramic gift, and like other holiday decorations I would take it out during the season, put it on a mantle or a shelf, and honestly not think that much more about it until it was time to put it away. Like those chess pieces it was stored in so many closets.

However, when Mom died, all those items — those pieces of her, those things that she had touched — came to mean so much more.

So, one year I pulled that ceramic Christmas tree out and placed it on the kitchen counter in its regular spot, and after the holidays, when all the other decorations went back into hibernation, I thought, "I'm going to keep this one out just a little longer."

Just a little longer turned into a lot longer. January turned into February turned into July turned into the next Christmas turned into the next January turned into … every … single … day.

Nowadays — years later — it's every bit as much of the kitchen decor as the microwave, the coffee maker and the fruit bowl. Often, when someone comes to the house for the first time, they'll see that little ceramic Christmas tree in our kitchen and tease us.

"Hey, it's July and you've still got your Christmas tree out … you must have forgotten to put it away."

Nope. I haven't forgotten. I'll never forget.

And I also know that Mom hasn't forgotten us; she's still looking over us. My wife would tell you that I'm not one who really believes in spirits or guardian angels. Jan does, but I don't.

Consider this tale, however:

A few years ago, we drove to my sister Lisa's house on the afternoon of Christmas Eve. She lived in Baldwinsville, New York, at the time. Like in most Italian families, Christmas Eve is big in ours; we used to gather at Mom and Dad's house, but after Mom died and it became too difficult for Dad to handle, we switched the venue to Lisa's for our celebration.

The day was clear and relatively warm for Dec. 24 as we headed east on the New York State Thruway. With no snow on the ground, we lamented the fact that it probably was going to be a green Christmas.

As we settled in at my sister's to eat dinner, though, it began snowing — those big, fluffy, lake effect flakes that are about the size of potato chips though softer than marshmallows.

Well, what do you know? It looked like it might be a white Christmas after all.

As we finished dinner and moved on to dessert, it kept snowing.

After coffee, it was time for the family gift exchange. And it kept snowing … by then it was starting to pile up, too.

After gifts, Dad — as tradition calls — started singing, "Pepino the Italian Mouse," "Dominick the Donkey," you know, the classics. And it kept snowing … and piling up … and by then, the wind was blowing, too.

You get the gist.

So, at an earlier-than-usual time, Jan and I made the call that it would be prudent to leave the festivities and make our way back to Geneva before the roads became totally unpassable, which, by the way, they would be by around midnight.

We again took the Thruway, which was almost completely barren of any other cars in either direction. The snow was still falling heavily, but the road surface didn't seem too bad. I was driving cautiously, going only about 45 mph, when — about eight or nine miles into our trek — we unsuspectingly cruised over a patch of black ice.

Almost immediately I could feel that I was losing control of the car, so I quickly took my foot off the gas. I also resisted the urge to pounce on the brakes, as I remembered being taught way back when in driver's ed class. I also tried to steer gently against whichever way the car wanted to go, another driver's ed tip.

I could tell, though, that we were sliding and were going to drift off the left shoulder. I told Jan to hold on because I didn't know where we were going to end up.

There was no guardrail on the left side, just a little slope that went down into a gully of a median. Our car came to rest — softly, I must say — on the downslope in about seven or eight inches of snow.

(It's funny, too, what you remember in situations like that. My first thought was of the man who taught those driver's ed classes all those years ago, a teacher named Chuck Wiltsie. He told us, "The statistics say that almost all of you will have an accident some day in your driving life; my job is to teach you how to make sure it's minor." Try telling a bunch of precocious, know-it-all teenagers that they are going to have an accident some day and you'll get the same snickering response that Chuck got from us: "Yeah, right." Except that after that accident, I silently thanked Chuck because all the lessons learned allowed me to, indeed, keep the incident minor. Others might say my Guardian Angel was a key).

Back to the car in the snow.

After we both calmed down and our heartbeats returned to normal, I called Triple A, while Jan called another roadside assistance outfit.

We both got the same answer: Sit tight, it's Christmas Eve and with the volume of cars that had slid off roads, it literally could be hours before help reached us.

Because the engine never quit, we had heat, so I decided, with Jan inside steering, that I would try to push the car up to the road. The snow was slippery and icy, but I actually managed to nudge it a bit, so I knew it wasn't stuck badly. If only I had another set of hands...

The male voice startled me.

"Hey, I was walking on the road up there, saw you guys slide and came down to help," the young man said. "Is there anything I can do?"

It was pitch dark, with heavy snow falling. The road he said he was walking on was probably six or seven football fields away with a snow-covered field, a forest of trees and a chain-link fence in between. I wondered how he possibly could have seen our incident. He wore a thin jacket over a T-shirt, jeans with a hole in one of the knees and sneakers, hardly attire to be taking a late-night stroll on that blustery, snowy Christmas Eve.

I wanted to say, "Where did you come from?" but instead told him he was a godsend and that I thought the two of us — again with my wife at the wheel — could probably push the car back up to the road level.

"Let's do it then," he said.

It took only one real good heave from our two-man unit working as a team to get it up to the shoulder. I looked the car over, saw absolutely no scratches or dents (again, thank you, Mr. Wiltsie ... and Mom), and turned to our benefactor.

"I can't thank you enough," I said, reaching for my wallet. I pulled out a $20 bill to give to him, but he waved it off.

I noticed again the rip in his jeans, and he said he had snagged them on that chain-link fence while he was climbing over it to come to our aid. Neither Jan nor I had seen anyone climbing over any chain-link fence, by the way.

"Please take the money and at least buy a new pair of jeans," I said. "You ripped them while coming to help us."

Again, he refused, and then he said, "If I were in the same situation, would you help me?"

"Yes, of course I would," I replied.

"I know you would," he said, walking away. "Merry Christmas."

I wished him the same and got back in the car, but Jan insisted that I try one more time to give him some money for his troubles.

I'd only been in the car for a handful of seconds, but when I got out to talk to him again, he was gone, absolutely nowhere to be seen. I looked to the fence … and past it to the field. No one, nothing. In fact, not even a sign of anyone.

And when I looked down to the snow-covered ground in the direction in which he had walked off I noticed the most astounding thing: There were no footprints!

Where had he come from? Where did he go?

Jan was convinced Mom sent him. Me? All I could hear was more Twilight Zone music.

In our family, if you'll indulge my use of newspaper metaphors, my Dad would be the headline – big and bold and full of punchy impact; Mom would have been the paragraph about halfway through the news story that explained, in a reserved, thoughtful way, what the whole thing was about, that would have made you say, "Ahhhh, now I understand." It's often called the "nut graph" in the business.

Not flashy. Definitely not punchy. But enlightening.

Dad was famous for his big bashes for family and friends, especially around the holidays. There was an abundance of food, free-flowing wine, singing and laughing. Mom was always there in the background, quietly and efficiently swapping out dishes in between courses, mopping up spilled *vino*, making sure everyone had what they needed and adding her own tale about family history whenever Dad took a breather.

You know what? After Mom died, those parties did, too. Dad is still around – still with a dynamic zest for life and an appetite for a good party – but his sidekick is gone. We only realize now what a great facilitator Mom was. Not necessarily the life of the party but the lifeblood of the party.

I could go on. And so could you about your Mom. But I will leave you with this: Mom was not much of a drinker but every once in a while, she liked a nip of Strega, the bright yellow herbal liqueur famous in southern Italy from the city of Benevento; now, whenever we gather for family functions, we end the festivities with a toast of Strega to her.

Mamma, grazie di tutto.

My Grandfather Luigi Adolfo Cutillo and my Grandmother Teresa Ereditario Cutillo relax on a bench outside their home in the village of San Salvatore Telesino. The school behind them is where my Dad took classes, until dropping out after the fourth grade so he could help his parents on the farm.

My Grandfather Adolfo explains the meaning of life to me – all in his native dialect – his very touristy-attired Grandson who understood proper Italian but not so much the dialect of the village.

5

The Meaning of Life, with Mio Nonno

Il savio non s'imbarca senza biscotto. – *Italian proverb*

Literally: A wise man does not get on the ship without a biscuit. In other words, always be prepared, one of the keys to life.

My Grandfather, Luigi Adolfo, was not exactly a world traveler. My Dad told me once that even though their village was only about 120 miles south of Rome, *nonno* never went to the Eternal City because it was simply too far, and he had no desire to see it. He was a farmer, not a sightseer, and in his day, one didn't venture too far from one's village or one's farm. So, when his son set off for America in 1958 to establish his family, *nonno* stayed put in Italy along with *nonna* Teresa.

That being the case, I only got to spend time with *nonno* on four occasions – twice when he visited us in the United States and twice when I visited him in Italy. I saw my *nonna* even less – just two times before she died in 1980. However, all of those special visits remain etched in my mind like they happened yesterday.

Their first trip to America – and I can only imagine how much this was a trip they never ever envisioned themselves making – was in 1962. I was all of two years old, but I remember the gigantic wooden airplane *nonno* made for me. I could sit on it and pretend I was flying anywhere in the world, though of course, at the princely age of two, my knowledge of that world was decidedly ... well, limited.

Didn't matter. My *nonno* had made that plane for me, and THAT'S what counted. It also didn't matter, decades later, when my Dad broke the news to me as an adult that the wooden airplane wasn't nearly as grandiose as it had been in my memory. *Nonno* had made it out of a couple of 4-by-4s that were about two feet long, Dad said. But hey, to a two-year-old that plane was as big as a 747.

What shocked my Dad, though, was that I even remembered that airplane at all. Indeed, it is probably the oldest memory – of *anything* – that I have. That must have been the effect that my *nonno* had on me. Or the airplane that he built had on me.

Another fun story came out of that trip, though it is not one that I witnessed. It is one that Dad remembers.

Mom and Dad had bought a nice piece of property in a residential neighborhood in the Lakeland area of Syracuse and had a foundation poured for what would be their first new home as a married couple. Dad was building the rest of the house with his own hands, little by little, mostly on the weekends and in the evenings after work at his real job, welding and cutting steel in a machine shop.

While his father was visiting, Dad asked him if he would like to work on landscaping the property, and my *nonno*, bored with just sitting around the house with the women all day while Dad was at work, jumped at the opportunity.

So every morning, while Dad would pack a lunch for himself in his metallic lunch box, he also would fix up a brown paper bag lunch for his father – leftovers from dinner the night before and of course, some wine. They would climb into the car together and drive off to the site of what would be our new home. Dad would drop him off there and head on into the city of Syracuse to put in his day's work at the factory. My *nonno* would spend the day attending to the property's plants, trees, lawn and flowers, planting some, clipping and pruning others, making everything look just so. He would eat his lunch at noon and even take a little nap on the lush green lawn in the early afternoon before getting back to his landscaping while waiting for his son to come and pick him up.

When Dad's workday concluded, he would drive back to the property, collect his father and together they would head on back to the farmhouse out in the country where the family was living until the new home was finished.

As many of you can attest, our Italian forefathers and foremothers could grow anything anywhere – tomatoes, garlic, peach trees, grapes, eggplant, basil, you name it. That much is no secret, but apparently the plants and foliage and greenery around that Lakeland property flourished so much under *nonno's* attentive care that one day, one of the neighbors on a more established property tracked down my Dad and said, "Hey, where did you get that gardener who works on your property every day? I'd like to hire him to do some work for me."

Probably sounding a little like Groucho Marx delivering a punchline, Dad replied: "That's no gardener. That's my father!"

The neighbor was astounded but still wanted to know if he was available to do some extra work. Dad thanked him but said no that wouldn't be possible.

The only time I ever was able to visit my grandmother and grandfather in Italy when they both were alive was in 1974 when Dad took me and my sister Teresa – guess who she was named after? – to the Old Country. I was 14 and Teresa was 12. My Zio Enzo, who I was meeting for the first time on that trip, picked us up at the Naples airport in his little Fiat and drove us wildly to their village of San Salvatore Telesino, about 45 minutes away (probably further, actually, but not with Zio "Mario Andretti" Enzo at the wheel). When I say "wildly," I mean that my uncle drove like many Italians in those days, as if he was in a passion play. He was constantly beeping the car's horn, flashing the lights – even in daylight – passing other cars at what seemed like the speed of light, zigging and zagging in the traffic like he was driving in a Formula One race. To my sister and me, it was invigorating, exhilarating, exciting – and hair raising – all at the same time.

Anyway, I will never forget as we pulled into the village and onto my grandparents' street, and the two of them were leaning out of the first-floor living room window waving to us as my *zio* drove the car up on the sidewalk right next to them. When I say up on the sidewalk, I mean when he screeched to a halt, my sister and I could lean out of the car's window and grasp our grandparents' hands. That was our Welcome to San Salvatore Telesino moment, and I'll never forget the smiles on my grandparents' faces.

I'll also never forget the $100 – in $5 American bills – that my *nonno* gave to me and to my sister on that trip, telling us, when we got back to America, to buy ourselves new bicycles. One hundred dollars was a lot of money in those days but where the money came from is the real story here. Dad, whenever he wrote a letter to his parents, which was fairly often in those days, would slip a $5 bill into the envelope for them along with the letter. The "bike money" that they gifted to Teresa and me was made up of those $5 bills, 40 of them from 40 different letters home from their son.

We only knew that because Dad had asked them where they got all that American money, and *nonno* told him, "From your letters!"

"From my letters? What?" Dad said. "That money was supposed to help you pay some bills. Why didn't you spend it?"

"We didn't need it, son, and besides, we would have had to go to the bank and change it to Italian *lira* before we could spend it. Too much trouble. So we just saved it," *nonno* said.

So, on that trip, they regifted it to Teresa and me, and when we returned to America we bought the fanciest, shiniest stingray bicycles that money could buy – correction: That Dad's money could buy.

Nonna Teresa died in 1980, and the next time – the only other time – *nonno* came to America was a few short years after that, in 1982. He was going to stay for six months through Christmas with my parents, but he ended up heading back to Italy after just two months because, again, he was just too bored most days, and there was no property in Lakeland to landscape. Mom and Dad worked all day, my sisters were in school, and I was away at college. *Nonno* couldn't watch television because he didn't understand a lick of English; he tried to watch American football one day, a sport he had never seen before, and told my father later, "I watched a sport that looked like war!" The first couple of days he didn't even know how to make himself coffee because he couldn't figure out how to operate the electric stove. When he announced that he thought he was going to leave much earlier than anticipated, he told my Dad, "*Sono solamente io e il gatto tutti i giorni ... e il gatto non mi capisce!*" It's only me and the cat every day, and the cat doesn't understand me!

"It's just me and the cat" became a running joke in our family.

We were incredibly sad to see *nonno* leave, but we understood. His life was in San Salvatore Telesino, even without *nonna*, so that is where he went to spend the rest of his time on earth.

As *nonno* grew older and more unable to take care of himself, especially without his wife, the talk, like in so many households, became how to care for him. Or more precisely, who could care for him. His one son lived in America, and his other was active in the military. Dad and Zio Enzo ended up making arrangements with their dear friend, Antonio DiPalma, and Antonio's family took *nonno* in for the final months of his life, which, because of the unbridled love Antonio's family had for him, turned out to be a magnificently wonderful and sweet time.

A few years after *nonno* died, in fact, a bunch of us were at Antonio's house – and there are always a bunch of people at Antonio's house, kids, grandkids, spouses, in-laws, friends, farmhands, etc. – and we started reminiscing about *nonno*. Antonio told the story about how they used to play cards every night with my grandfather, who was quite a card player. In his final months, he was in a wheelchair, though, and the arms of that wheelchair butted against the table ledge so that my grandfather could not get close enough to the table to comfortably lay his cards down. Antonio, incredible loving gentleman that he was, rectified that. He sawed out a piece of that beautiful wooden dining room table so that my grandfather could roll his wheelchair right up in there.

I almost couldn't believe that tale, which brought tears to my eyes, and Antonio told me to come with him into another room. He told me that very table was still there, and he pointed it out to me. It was covered by a white linen tablecloth, but Antonio showed me the spot at the table where *nonno* always sat, and then he lifted the tablecloth to reveal the cutout spot for him and his wheelchair.

That is when the tears really started rolling down my cheeks. They were heartfelt tears of joy generated by Antonio's compassionate and loving treatment of my grandfather.

I mean, who saws a notch out of their beautiful wooden dining room table so that an old man can play cards?

Who, besides Antonio, that is?

The last time I saw *nonno* was in the summer of 1990. He would die the following spring, finally reunited with *nonna* Teresa. I was excited to see him that summer because I thought I had learned enough Italian in college to finally be able to have a great conversation with him, other than "Hello, Joe." I remember sitting in the courtyard of the family farmhouse just outside the village. Even though he had a home in the village, he also kept that old farmhouse, which is where he made and stored his wine, cured his meats and cheeses, and dried his herbs and tomatoes. We were sitting in rickety wooden chairs that barely supported me, at least – my grandfather being considerably smaller than me, didn't have a problem. He poured some of that homemade red *vino* into small glasses, and I was so thrilled to get into a deep discussion about all kinds of fabulous things … my father growing up … the village in the old days … his life with *nonna* … Italy in the old days. But when *nonno* started talking, I quickly realized there was an issue I hadn't considered – he only spoke dialect, as most of the other folks of his generation did back then. I, on the other hand, had been schooled in proper Italian, the Florentine dialect. So, here we were, book-educated grandson and dialect-speaking grandfather, and we were *still* unable to converse fluently. But you know what? It was one of the greatest conversations of my life, one that I will never forget. I tossed a few words in here and there that I knew he could understand, asked a few questions and just let him carry the dialogue, even though I could understand very little of it.

It really didn't matter because I'm quite sure he told me the meaning of life that day. And even if he didn't, the sun was shining, the birds were chirping, the *vino* was going down very smoothly, and I was hanging with my *nonno*.

What could have been better?

6

To Zio Enzo -
'Hip, Hip, Hip, Hoorah!'

La vita è un'opportunità, coglila. ... La vita è bellezza, ammirala. ... La vita è un sogno, fanne una realtà. ... La vita è amore, godine. ... La vita è un mistero, scoprilo. ... La vita è un inno, cantalo. ... La vita è un'avventura, rischiala. ... La vita è felicità, meritala. ... La vita è la vita, difendila.

> *– "La Vita" di Madre Teresa di Calcutta*

Literally: Life is an opportunity, benefit from it. ... Life is beauty, admire it. ... Life is a dream, make it a reality. ... Life is love, enjoy it. ... Life is a mystery, discover it. ... Life is a hymn, sing it. ... Life is an adventure, dare it. ... Life is happiness, deserve it. ... Life is life, defend it.

> *– Excerpts from "Life" by Mother Teresa of Calcutta*

Dad, my Uncle Vincenzo, and my buddy Steve Venuti were relaxing in the side yard of my uncle's villa, built on incredibly fertile farmland that my grandfather had once owned, and his father before him. They sat around a small white plastic table upon which rested a bottle of homemade white wine and three small glasses. The gentle summer breeze was perfumed by fruit from nearby trees in the villa's front yard – apricots, prickly pears, peaches and cherries.

"*Pollice,*" Zio Enzo said, looking at Steve and holding up his thumb, which is what the word means.

"*Pollice,*" Steve repeated.

"*Indice,*" Zio said with his index finger held up.

"*Indice,*" Steve said.

"*Medio,*" Zio said, shooting up his middle finger in what some would see as a vulgar gesture. But not in this context.

"*Medio,*" Steve repeated.

"*Anulare,*" Zio said with his ring finger extended.

"*Anulare,*" my friend repeated.

"*Mignolo,*" Zio said, sticking out his pinky finger.

"*Mignolo,*" Steve said.

"*Bravo!*" my uncle said before reciting the names of all five digits in rapid-fire succession: "*Pollice ... indice ... medio ... anulare ... mignolo.*" As he did, he shot out each of the fingers he was announcing until all five were extended and he was able to wiggle a palm full of fingers at Steve.

Steve did the same, extending his five fingers as he repeated: "*Pollice ... indice ... medio ... anulare ... mignolo.*"

"*Bravo,*" Zio Enzo practically shouted. "*Bravissimo!*"

All three men laughed, took a sip of the white wine in the glasses in front of them, leaned back in their chairs and let the summer fruit-infused breeze wash over them. A few minutes of regular conversation — in Italian between my Zio and my Dad — followed, and then Zio, feeling that Steve was either getting bored or perhaps just needed another lesson of reinforcement, would start it all again by thrusting out that thumb.

"*Pollice,*" he commenced ... and off they went again down the road of Learning the Names of the Fingers in Italian.

It reminded me very much of Apollonia in "The Godfather," claiming to her new husband Michael Corleone that she knew English very well and that she would prove it by reciting the days of the week, though she did so in the incorrect order: "*Monday, Tuesday, Thursday, Wednesday, Friday, Sunday, Saturday ...*"

In this case, though, it had nothing to do with Marlon Brando or Mario Puzo. It was my very own Zio Enzo Cutillo making another trip – this trip in particular – a little extra special. This passion play was in 2010, and my buddy Steve had escorted my Dad to the Old Country because Dad couldn't travel on his own. I didn't have nearly as much vacation time as Steve or Dad, both of whom were retired – or on "permanent vacation" as Dad likes to call it. I arrived about five days after them, and in those first five days, Zio Enzo had – as usual – put his stamp on this trip, as he always did.

I was a newcomer – or in this case, a late comer – to this party. Whatever the case, in the days leading up to my arrival Zio Enzo had decided that he was going to teach the American, who knew a little bit of Italian but not much, the names of the fingers. And quite emphatically so. That became the theme of the 2010 trip, and every time we had a few extra minutes – especially in the middle of the hot afternoons just before or after nap time – Zio was going to make sure that Steve got in his repetitions, starting with "*pollice ...*"

My uncle did something similar on almost every trip I've ever made to visit him, making each one extra special.

In 1990, Dad, another buddy, Ken Boyd, and I went to Italy to visit and to catch some World Cup soccer games. Dad and my flight from Syracuse was delayed a day by thunderstorms, but Ken was departing from New York City where flights were not delayed, so he needed to go on without us or lose his non-refundable ticket. Zio Enzo had never met Ken but was tasked with picking the American up at the Naples Airport. Not sure how he would recognize him, Zio used all his military training and influence and as Ken says, "He mobilized the entire police force and the military to be on the lookout for me when I got off the plane." Boyd being an odd name for the Italian tongue, Zio had a number of signs made up with what he thought was the proper spelling, "Mr. BOID," and had all the cops chirping "Mr. Boid ... Mr. Boid ... Mr. Boid" as Ken walked through the terminal. This was long before it became a common practice for every taxi driver, Uber driver and hotel limo driver to bombard passengers with these types of signs, so Zio was not only ahead of his time, but the "Mr. Boid" story became legendary in San Salvatore Telesino as it was told at every home we visited on that trip, usually over a few glasses of wine and accompanied by cat calls and Mr. Boids.

Another time, my sister Lisa and her husband at the time, Dwayne, traveled with us. My uncle did not quite get that name of Irish and Gaelic origin. He would shrivel up his nose and in a real nasally voice say,

Vincenzo Cutillo, my Dad's only brother, was a career military man in the Italian Army.

"Dwaaaaaaayne" – emphasis on the long A sound. He did that often in the early days of that visit but relatively quickly decided that he needed to "Italo-cize" – which is quite different from "italicize" – that Anglo name. Because there is no name that translates into Dwayne in Italian, he dubbed him Duilio – pronounced DWEEL-e-o. It's a name that, as far as my research can ascertain, translates to, well, Duilio, and that's about it. Supposedly, it dates back to a third century Roman politician who went by Gaius Duilius. But for our trip – and yes, for posterity – Dwayne became Duilio. And when we returned to America and were able to "English-cize" it back, it became, simply, Dweels.

Thank you for that, Uncle Vince.

Another time, Zio had two young, energetic dogs that I am quite sure had been bestowed with Italian names. But when my 10-year-old daughter Kristine fell in love with the pups and asked Zio Enzo what their names were, he said, "Happy," I'm sure for the sake of his young American grandniece. She loved it, and when she asked, with a bright contented smile, what the *other* puppy's name was, he said, again, "Happy."

Could they really both be Happy, she wondered? I asked him in Italian.

"Yes," Zio Enzo replied with a smile that was equally as bright as hers. "Happy 1 and Happy 2."

So, for the rest of that trip, my young daughter – an only child who had to endure traveling with six adults for most of that excursion – was able to live a child's carefree, gleeful, merry life, running around the villa's property and playing with Happy 1 and Happy 2.

Zio Enzo was a special man, and he had that effect on people. Like my grandfather, he spoke only a few words of English, though he probably knew more than he let on. Those that he did use, however, became his calling cards. His favorite phrase was "Number one!" and he would say it enthusiastically and with his thumb – or *pollice* – extended.

"What do you think about that plate of macaroni, Zio?"

"It's Number One!!!!" he would reply with his customary gusto.

"Hey, Zio Enzo, what do you think about these peaches I plucked off the trees in your backyard?"

"Number One!!!!" he exclaimed.

He also liked the phrase "Happy Days," and yes, whether you were a fan or not, it came from the Arthur Fonzarelli-inspired American sitcom of the same name. When we were all together, and especially if there were other Americans in the room, such as me or my sisters or friends, he loved popping open a bottle of sparkling Prosecco wine or Spumante and bellowing "Here we go … Happy Days!!!!"

Zio Enzo was born in 1927, four years before Dad, his only sibling, which made for an unusually small Italian nuclear family back at that time. Don't fret for the Cutillos, though, and our family tree: their father had five brothers and two sisters, their mother had four brothers and a sister, and my mother's father, Dominic Tucci, had seven brothers and four sisters! There are dozens and dozens of branches on that tree … and equally as many cousins.

But in the Cutillo family of Adolfo and Teresa, there were only two boys, and in fact, those two boys didn't even really grow up together. Young Enzo had a penchant for school and a thirst for knowledge and studies. Because their small farming village didn't even have a secondary school, Enzo's mother decided early on that he should go live with her sister in the nearby city of Caserta, which had better schools and more opportunities for a bright young student. Her sister, Filomena, was married twice – her first husband, Angelo, died in the Spanish Civil War in 1937 – but she could not have children of her own, so Enzo went to live with her while his brother Michele, my Dad, stayed back in the village. Dad, whose passion was playing soccer, attended school only through the primary grades, then spent the rest of his time kicking the ball around and helping his parents out on the family farm.

Zio Enzo, like Dad, lived through World War II and was intrigued by the military maneuvering, so much so that when he received his high school diploma in 1947, he decided to pursue a career in the Italian Army. He was accepted into the military academy in the northern city of Modena, not an easy feat, especially for a young man from the poor south of Italy. He studied there for two years, concentrating on military tactics. After that, he was sent to Venaria Reale in the Piedmont, near the car-manufacturing city of Torino, where he continued to learn about commanding men and leading troops.

His itinerary also included assignments in Naples and in Rome at Cecchignola, a self-contained military area that was closed off to the public. As he studied and learned, he also moved up the ranks, first being made a captain and then in 1965, at the age of 38, being promoted to colonel. At the time, he was the youngest colonel in the Italian Army, a fact of which he was always extremely proud.

As fate would have it, he eventually was assigned to command a base in Caserta – where his love for school had been formulated while living as a child with his Zia Filomena. The first time I ever met him, in 1974, he arranged for my Dad and me to sleep on the base there with other soldiers, which I thought was about the coolest thing in the world. Only sleeping in the same room with the New York Yankees would have been better for a 14-year-old boy at that time.

Zio Enzo served as a colonel until 1988 when he retired at the mandatory age of 60. Just before his retirement, however, in what was the proudest accomplishment of his life, he was promoted to the rank of general, which came with commendations, letters and certificates signed by the highest-ranking military and political figures in Italy, including the president, Francesco Cossiga. He also received a general's full regalia and uniform.

After retiring, he and his wife Rita, a teacher, continued to live in Caserta, but he also spent as much time as possible in the country villa that he had built just outside of San Salvatore Telesino, and whenever he went back there – for holidays, family gatherings or even just to tend to the yard – he was looked upon with reverence by the villagers, most of whom called him *"Colonello"* out of respect, since that was the rank that he had held for the longest time. A few villagers, primarily those who didn't know him as well, called him *"Generale"* and looked up to him as the only native son of San Salvatore Telesino to rise to the rank of general in the Italian Army.

Despite all the accolades, the awards, and the certificates, though, he also was simply my Dad's big brother, and even though they didn't

At a restaurant in Tuscany, Zio Enzo, my Dad, and their best friend Antonio,
steal the show as "The Three Tenors."

spend an awful lot of time together in their youthful age, they made up
for it later in life. Zio Enzo also brought that forceful, demonstrative –
but always engaging – military fervor with him to all family gatherings,
along with that ever-present twinkle in his eye. That was part of the fun
of being around him.

At every family get together, Zio Enzo – sitting at his rightful
place at the head of the table, even when it wasn't at his home – would
recite poetry (he loved Mother Teresa of Calcutta's poem about life,
which begins this chapter), tell a joke or a story or two, or sing, very
loudly and very proudly. I don't know how family dinners commence
in your house, but with Zio Enzo at the table, no one ate until he belted
out *"Il Canto degli Italiani,"* otherwise known as Italy's national anthem.
After dinner, especially if my Dad was at the table with him, they would
sing other more fun Italian tunes, such as a drinking song called *"Beviam,*
Beviam, Beviamo" or the more traditional *"O Sole Mio"* or *"Santa Lucia,"* or
even songs made popular by Italian-American crooners such as Dean
Martin or Frank Sinatra.

All the while, Zio Enzo would accentuate the festivities with a military-like pound of the fist on the table that would make all the glasses jump or a long – and boisterous – final few notes of every song.

And while the dinner or lunch or brunch or whatever it was progressed, Zio would think of reasons to offer a toast, and he would do so with a very exuberant "Hip, hip, hip … hoorah!!" – repeated, always, three times, by the way. That may seem trite to American readers but was as sincere, as spirited, as heart-felt as anything you could imagine.

In 2002, when my cousin Claudio, Zio's grandson, celebrated his 18th birthday – an important one in the Italian tradition like Sweet 16 in America – I was fortunate enough to be at the restaurant in Caserta to party along with the family. We were at a table in a balcony overlooking the dance floor when we heard that dancing girls – belly dancers, in fact – were going to be coming out to perform for Claudio. When we heard a commotion down below us, we looked from our perch to check out the festivities and who should be right in the middle of those dancers, shimmying along with them?

Yes, the Generale. Or the Colonello.

He also endeared himself to a number of the folks that I brought to Italy on group trips in later years. In 2009, I took a group of 50 or so friends on a tour of Tuscany, and Zio Enzo came to our going away dinner, escorted by the two brothers' best friend, Antonio DiPalma. The festivities were held in a small Tuscan restaurant near San Gimignano, complete with musician/singer Federico Tozzi, who brought with him a karaoke machine. Dominating the singing that night? Yes, primarily Zio Enzo, accompanied every other song or two by Dad and by Antonio; they were dubbed the Three Tenors. It was such a raucous evening that even the wait staff of the restaurant pulled back from their serving duties to just hang out and watch, with broad smiles on their faces, as the Italian *"tre tenori"* entertained the American tourists.

Another group venture was to the Amalfi Coast in 2011 and again, my Dad accompanied us to a certain point and then went off to visit his brother while we completed our trip. At the final farewell dinner, Zio brought Dad to our hotel in the lovely Amalfi town of Maiori where our dinner was hosted by a restaurant that didn't want a band or the crazy shenanigans of the Tuscan place in 2009 because they had other customers trying to enjoy a quiet evening meal. Didn't matter to Zio Enzo. He brought his daughter Anna and her husband Angelo, *amico* Antonio and his wife Maria, and my Dad to the restaurant and once the eating was finished, the floor show began. They didn't need musical instruments to accompany them on *"Volare"* and *"Eh Cumpari"* and other rollicking Italian songs. That, friends, is how memories are made.

To this day, the folks on those trips – who loved every bit of the sightseeing, wine drinking and Italy exploring that we did – say the highlight was enjoying the Two Brothers.

Sadly, Zio Enzo was able to visit the United States only one time, and that was in 2008, the summer after our mother died. He came to make sure that his brother, an unexpected widower, was handling it OK, along with the rest of us. While Dad traveled back to Italy over 50 times – I often joked with him that it must have set some kind of record – my uncle, when he was active in the Army was not allowed to go anywhere as far as America. Then, by the time he retired in '88, his wife was unable to travel much. So he made that one trip only … but he made that one special too.

While visiting with all of us on that sad but still uplifting occasion, a song made famous in 1965 by an Italian crooner named Adriano Celentano – *"Grazie, Prego, Scusi* (or "Thank You, Your Welcome, Excuse Me") – somehow or another became the theme, Zio Enzo's calling card for that three-week period. He pulled it out and made a big deal of it whenever he had a chance for all of us, my sisters, my wife, my daughter, his brother.

"Grazie, Prego, Scusi" was the name of the song and the refrain. But the next word in it was *"Tornerò"* – I'll be back. He never did come back, but it didn't matter because he had left his mark.

He was a special man, I'll say it again, and if you noticed that I used the past tense in describing Zio Enzo, it is because he has indeed passed away, in fact, as this book was being written in 2018. He died at the ripe, young age of 91 on Sept. 4, and I was in Italy two days later to pay my respects and to say *"Ci vediamo"* to my *bellissimo* Zio, a man who could command not only a platoon of soldiers but also any dining room that I've ever seen.

I will miss him, but every April 5, when I celebrate my birthday, I will have a special "Hip hip, hip, hoorah!" in his honor. Three times, of course. Because that day – April 5, my birthday – was his birthday too.

7

Remembering
Zio 'al Fondo'

Non è mai troppo saggio il parere preso al fondo di più d'un bicchiere.
– Italian proverb

Literally: The opinion taken at the bottom of more than one glass is never too wise. *(Or, the more glasses of wine you drink, the more your reasoning will be cloudy.)*

The generally accepted definition for "Renaissance Man" is a person with a variety of skills and a broad base of knowledge. Leonardo da Vinci – an actual man from the actual Renaissance – is considered the archetype of the term, a man of many talents with what has been described as an "unquenchable curiosity."

When you think of Da Vinci, you think of the arts and science and mathematics. When I think of the Renaissance man in my family, I think of basket weaving, mushrooms and limoncello.

Allow me to elaborate.

Zio Salvatore Cutillo was not really my "*zio*" – or uncle – but was my Dad's cousin, and really more like a brother. He and Dad grew up together, they played together, they got into mischief together, they ate chestnuts together. I just called him *zio* out of respect.

But here is what the man could do:

Limoncello? He made the best I have ever tasted, starting, of course, with the sweetest lemons that grew to be the size of small footballs on trees in his front yard. Pluck those babies off the trees, skin off the zest, add sugar and alcohol and he had limoncello. Zio Salvatore always had a bottle – or three – in the freezer ready for any occasion.

Zio doing an "al fondo" among some of the baskets he had woven and wine he had made.

Mushrooms? He knew just the right time to go out and collect them, and he knew just the right ones to pick – late fall, a nip in the air, Zio Salvatore would take a few baskets and go out to the base of a small mountain near the village. He would spend all day out there and return with baskets filled with *porcini*, the most luscious I've ever tasted.

Cheese? He didn't make it himself, but he knew the directions up the winding mountain roads to the home of the family that made the best fresh pecorino you have ever had. One of Dad's first phone calls any time we visited the village was to his cousin Salvatore to make sure that he could arrange a cheese-buying expedition.

Baskets? Speaking of those, this was something I learned only recently: he weaved his own. First, he would go out into the wild and collect the willow reeds. He would take them home, dry them, and then weave them into unbelievably gorgeous and intricate baskets, including incredibly ornate baptismal baskets that he would give as gifts to new parents. The only time my wife ever met Zio Salvatore, she was so enamored with his weaving work that he gave her two gifts – a small flower basket and a flat woven piece that she uses for bread. She careful-ly packed the flat one in her suitcase like it was a million-dollar piece of art – a Da Vinci perhaps? – and she carried the small basket on her arm the entire trip back to America.

Music? He was well into his 80s and still part of a small troupe that performed traditional Italian song and dance at festivals, parties, even simply in the town square on Friday nights. Dressed in colorful histori-cal garb, he usually played hand-held percussion type instruments. Heck, he probably made them himself.

Wine? The best homemade stuff I've ever had and plentiful, al-ways enough. One time I visited when he was in the early stages of mak-ing his wine for the year, and he was running it through a first fermen-tation in the largest plastic half-drum I had ever seen; it must have held 100 gallons of wine. I asked him why he made so much, was some of it to sell? And he shot me a look with furrowed eyebrows and said "Sell? This is wine for the family. Hey, it has to last the whole year."

He built wood-burning brick ovens; he had one in his garage, and in fact, you pulled your car right up to it when you drove into that ga-rage. I often asked him if he would come to the United States and build me such an oven, and he said he would. All I needed to do was buy the materials and pay for his flight, and he would come and do it. I believe he would have, too, but we waited a little too long to pull the trigger on that idea.

He built houses – no easy feat in Italy where they are all made of cement and stone, not wood as in America. He raised chickens in that same garage, some for eating, some for eggs. And again, speaking of that all-purpose garage, he had all sorts of crops hanging from the beams – peppers, tomatoes, onions, garlic, herbs. You name it. He har-vested wild oregano, dried it and gave me plastic bags of it to bring home to America. If you like oregano in your pizza sauce – and really, who doesn't? – you haven't tasted anything until you tasted this stuff that was bitter, peppery and sweet all at the same time. Made his own olive oil, too, and I probably don't have to describe how luscious and smo-oth the stuff was.

Add that all up and it becomes MY definition of a Renaissance man. I tell you all this not so much to brag or shine the light just on Zio Salvatore, but because I'll bet most of you can think of someone in your family who was a true Renaissance man or woman in the same kind of well-rounded way.

But ... there's one more thing about my *zio* that I will remember as long as I live. He drank his wine *"al fondo,"* which means "to the last drop" or "to the bottom," sort of like our expression, "Bottoms up."

Check this out: I first noticed the routine decades ago as a precocious young American visitor. Zio Salvatore would fill up everyone's glass at the table, small 3-4 ounce juice glasses. He would proceed to drink his all down in one smooth gulp, while we would sip ours. He waited patiently until all our glasses were empty, no matter how long it took, and sometimes, as folks told stories and ate snacks, it would take something of a while. But when all those glasses were empty, he would fill them all up and again drink his all down in one pull and then patiently go about waiting for us to sip and empty ours over time. And so it would go. Over and over as long as the storytelling – and the *vino* – flowed.

I noticed this practice and finally asked my Dad what was up with Zio basically doing "shots" of wine. Dad told me, "Oh, that's how all the old-timers used to drink wine when they were sitting around telling stories. It's called 'al fondo,' to the last drop."

My Dad's father, Luigi Adolfo, drank his that way; Zio Salvatore's father, Antonio, drank his that way. All the aunts and uncles, that's how they consumed their *vino,* according to Dad.

Well, as you probably know, nicknames are popular in Italy, so from that point on, Zio Salvatore became Zio "al Fondo." My Dad would refer to him that way whenever he spoke to me about him, and it was very casual and matter-of-fact, sort of like, "Hey, Zio al Fondo told me he went out and picked a basket full of mushrooms the other day" or "Hey, your Zio al Fondo told me to tell you he is waiting for you to come to visit; he wants to do an *al fondo* with you."

It became a tradition every bit as important as going to get the cheese up in the mountains and going to pick mushrooms. When we would first arrive at Zio's house, we started the festivities by doing an "al fondo," and then – no matter how long the visit lasted – we would close those festivities by doing another "al fondo." And yes, sometimes we would even do a few in between.

We lost Zio Salvatore al Fondo in 2017, at the wonderful age of 88, a beautiful life. As my dad said, "The family lost a great, great father."

The first time I went to San Salvatore Telesino after he had left us, it seemed a bit surreal to not see him. But I stopped in at his son Raffaele's house, and of course, we did an "al fondo" in his honor. In fact, we did two of them – one at the beginning of the visit, and one, as tradition holds, at the end.

I also told Raffaele about how much my wife had loved Zio's baskets, and before I left that evening, he told me to hang on. He went back to another part of the house and brought out another of those flat bread baskets that Zio had woven. He told me, "This is the last one that he ever made; we have many of them to remember him by, but please take this one home to your wife. He would be happy that she had it."

I didn't want to accept it – the *last one* he ever made, are you kidding? – but of course, I did. I packed it carefully, too, just like she had the others years ago. It made it to America safely and hangs on our wall with the others.

And so, Zio, we think of you often whenever we look at those beautiful pieces that you created. I will miss you and I will keep your memories alive until we meet again and can do another "*al fondo!*"

IL MIO STILE DI VITA ITALIANA

MY ITALIAN LIFESTYLE

8

It's All About
The Food

Esse nu fesso chi dice male di macaroni. – *Centuries-old Neapolitan Proverb*
Literally: One has to be an idiot to speak badly of macaroni.

Amicizie e maccheroni, sone meglio caldi. – *Old Italian proverb*
Literally: Friendships and macaroni are best when they are warm.

Naturally, with a country like Italy, there are many, many proverbs and sayings that compare food to life, and the two at the beginning of this chapter are among my favorites.

I have used my newspaper columns over the years to write about eating in restaurants and in homes throughout Italy and about eating in restaurants in "Little Italys" around the United States.

I have mused about when it became vogue to call that stuff made out of semolina that we boil and eat with our favorite marinara sauce "pasta" rather than what it really is, "macaroni."

In our house growing up, Dad would make the sauce and then he would give us kids the choice of what he would cook to go with it, and the choices were simply these: *spaghetti* or *macaroni*.

Spaghetti, we all know what that is. Macaroni basically would be whatever we had in the cupboard. It could be *penne*, it could be *rigatoni*, it could be butterflies (*farfalle*), it could be what we called wagon wheels (*rotelle*), it could be spirals (*fusilli*). If it was *ziti*, that was extra fun because Dad always got the long, narrow tubes, and we would sit there and break them up into bite-size ziti pieces before he boiled them. But those were ALL macaroni.

Pasta? Not so much.

I also have written about olive groves and pecorino cheese, prosciutto and "meatless meatballs." Eating fish on Christmas Eve and great loaves of wood-burning, brick-oven-baked Italian bread.

Wait, what was that? Meatless meatballs? You don't know what those are?

Well, they are kind of a specialty of Dad's, though I'll bet that all Italian cooks have something like them in their repertoire. They have absolutely everything to do with meatballs – that is, they contain every ingredient that meatballs have – cheese, breadcrumbs, parsley and other herbs, eggs and whatever else you put in your meatballs – except for one rather important ingredient, MEAT. Dad remembers them as being called something like *pangotole* back in his mother's San Salvatorese dialect, but you won't find anything like that even with an internet search. In fact, it may actually be the only word – if it even is a word – that you can Google and find zero results. I'm serious. Zero. Try it.

Go ahead, I'll wait.

Because *pane* means bread in Italian, I kind of think it means "little bread balls … with all the ingredients of meatballs except the meat." Or something along those lines. Plus, my Dad may not even be remembering the name exactly correctly.

But, as he would say, whose care?

Anyway, I – and everyone in my family – call these melt-in-your-mouth concoctions "meatless meatballs," even though Dad cooks them in a loaf instead of balls. He mixes all the meatball ingredients – very heavy, by the way, on eggs – forms and presses them into a loaf, then fries the outside of it to a gorgeous golden-brown color in the best olive oil. Then he bakes the loaf so that it all stays together. What temperature? I don't know. This isn't a cookbook. Try 450° for 10 minutes. Or 300° at 30 minutes.

After baking, he lets it cool, and then he slices it up, maybe in half-inch thick pieces. Those pieces are cooked in the sauce. Just like using meatballs or sausage or any other meat, the *pangotole* flavor the sauce. They also soak it up like crazy.

This is the ultimate in *"la cucina povera,"* or poor man's cooking, for which so much of Italy is known. You know about pasta-and-beans – or pasta fazool – right? Poor man's meal. Greens and beans? Poor man's meal. Gizzards, if you like those. Even tripe (and if you don't know what that is, it's something that definitely *can* be found with a Google search). Anyway, you get the picture. All poor man's meals. When Dad was young his family rarely had any meat to put in meatballs, so his mother improvised this recipe to use all the other ingredients, which were abundant, and also to flavor the sauce.

I've made them over the years – nowhere near as well as Dad, believe me – and people SWEAR there is meat in them. There has to be, they say, to taste that good. No there doesn't. Trust me.

Pangotole. Or something like that.

So, basically this chapter is all about something that is near and dear to the hearts of all Italians and Italian-Americans, not to mention our waistlines: food.

It's one of the great things about having roots that trace back to that boot over there in the Mediterranean.

I come from a family where my Dad and my late great Uncle Joe Arduini would be sitting at the table eating breakfast and talking about what they were going to eat for lunch. Not just talking about it, having a full-out discussion over coffee.

At lunch time, they would discuss what they were going to eat for dinner.

And at dinner, quite naturally, they would figure out what leftovers they could save for tomorrow morning's breakfast *frittata*.

Does it get better than that? I don't think so, and I'll bet things happen similarly in your family.

Yes, the day's coming and goings, school and work, games and soap operas, shopping and cleaning, all were fashioned around – or punctuated by – what was on the table. And what would be on the NEXT day's table.

And so on.

Taking that a step further, we can be at a beautiful restaurant, enjoying a savory and delicious meal, and our conversation, invariably, will be about some other memorable meal we had at some other beautiful restaurant. Like, you're eating this exquisite veal piccata, but you're saying, "Hey, remember when we were in that little joint in the Upper East Side of Manhattan and we had that awesome garlic bread? That was unbelievable."

It's got nothing to do with the restaurant you're in. Nothing to do, even, with the city you're in. It's all about the company ... and the food.

My Dad has always been the cook in our family, and the ironic thing is that he never even knew he had it in him. He might have run by a pot of bubbling sauce that his mother was cooking, stuck a chunk of bread in it and bolted out the door on his way to some soccer game when he was a youngster, but he never really watched his parents cook, nor did he ask them for recipes, ingredients, techniques; nothing. There were no such things anyway.

But when he came to the United States in '58 and began longing for those traditional dishes of home – *pangotole* among others – he had to conjure them up himself. He had to rely on memories of the way his Mom would add a dash of oregano or his Dad would throw in a handful of basil and of course, untold taste tests and trials by error.

As he experimented and tweaked, he figured things out, boiling it all down to a pretty tasty science. My Uncle Louie used to say that Dad could cook a 2-by-4 and make it taste good.

And just as your Italian parents and grandparents, aunts and uncles, he uses no recipes. He could write his own cookbook, but I think the title would have to be "Cooking By Feel," and it wouldn't have any traditional recipes in it.

A number of years ago, my brother-in-law's mother was so taken by Dad's cooking that she asked if he could give her the recipes for a five-course meal he had just put on. When we got done laughing hysterically, he told her that he didn't use recipes. At first, she didn't believe him, but when we all vouched for the truthfulness of that, she asked, instead, if she might be able to spend a day with him as he prepared such a meal, from the planning to the shopping to the preparing to the cooking to the eating. She would watch, learn, observe, listen, taste and – most importantly – take down her own notes.

Dad, good-natured fellow that he is, agreed. So she did, indeed, spend a day with him as he went from start to finish on one of those memorable, multi-course masterpieces. She accompanied him to the grocery store as he bought everything for the meal, picking out the best meat, the freshest produce, the finest products all the way around.

She went back to the house with him and watched studiously as he laid everything out and went about making the meal, all the while asking questions and taking notes, copious notes.

A few weeks later, she attempted to recreate the exact same meal, and she reported to us that her notetaking must have been woefully insufficient because the food just didn't come out the way that Dad's had. She blamed it on the notes, but a little while later, my brother-in-law told us the real reason why the meal hadn't come out the same – his mother had made substitutions and changes to Dad's routine, cutting some corners, such as reducing the number of eggs for cholesterol reasons, using less cheese because it was too salty, adding more oregano because she liked it. Things like that.

When Dad heard that, he just shook his head, almost kind of sadly. Why did she bother, he asked? If you want to do it your own way, do it your own way, but it won't taste like mine.

Well, of course, we all know why she bothered ... because it is all about the food. Even if you don't have the feel for it.

Hey, what's cooking?

9

Even a Trip To Get
The Cheese Becomes
Memorable

Come il cacio sui maccheroni. – *Old Italian proverb*
Literally: Like cheese on macaroni. (Or, they go together perfectly)

My Zio Salvatore's 15-year-old Fiat Cinquecento plup-plup-plup-ped easily up the mountain – or up the "mount" in my Dad's broken English, if you've been following along. I was behind the wheel, working the well-broken-in, five-gear stick shift so that Zio and my father were free to talk without having to pay too much attention to the narrow, winding road or the donkeys that sometimes hung out so close to the side of that road that I had to be careful not to clip them as we plupped by them.

Of course, Zio Salvatore — who is really dad's cousin, but I call him uncle out of respect; you met him in an earlier chapter as well — was paying enough attention to chime out directions every few hundred yards, or so it seemed.

"*Gira qui,*" he would say, turn here. Or "*A sinistra,*" to the left. Even, "*No, hai perso il turno,*" no, you missed the turn.

I would turn, adjust or brake, accordingly, correct the Fiat's path, and we would continue the ascent.

We were heading up Mount Mutria, smallish as mountains go — not quite 6,000 feet in elevation. It is in the Province of Campobasso in the Matese mountain range, which is part of Italy's central-southern Apennines. It also is near Dad's village of San Salvatore Telesino.

This was a big day. No, make that A Big Day!!! It was Cheese Day, one of the happiest events during each of the numerous trips I have made to the Old Country with Dad. On this day, facilitated by Zio Salvatore, as tradition demands, we were heading to the small mountain commune of Pietraroja to buy homemade cheese to take back to America.

It's one of our routines that always plays out the same way: Whenever we arrive in the village, one of the first phone calls Dad makes is to his cousin Salvatore, and the first question he asks him is "When can we pick up the cheese?" Zio, in turn, phones his friends, cheese makers Angelo and Laura Bello, and arranges a day for us to visit their home up toward the top of that mountain to buy the wheels and bricks of that salty yet sweet homemade pecorino, which, in Italy is made from sheep's milk – *pecora*, in Italian, meaning sheep. Its savoriness is ideal when grated on top of a heap of spaghetti and sauce to bring out all their flavors.

So, on that particular sunny September day, we were doing what we often do, driving up the mountain roads. We were almost to the village — population, by the way, of 586 — when our path was blocked by hundreds of meandering sheep and a handful of dogs all led by a shepherd, a red-cheeked, robust, though weathered and hunched-over, man of about 70. When he saw our Fiat, he used a combination of his dogs and his staff, banging it on the road, to astonishingly "steer" the sheep to one side of the narrow road, forming one clear lane for our car to pass. We inched past slowly, and then Zio Salvatore asked me to stop. His 85-year-old memory failing a bit as to exactly where the Bellos lived, he wanted to ask the shepherd, figuring that such a man in these parts quite probably knew all 586 of those residents. Thankfully, he did know the Bellos and gave us directions to their home, noting that it was near the center of the tiny village, just off the piazza of the church of Santa Maria Assunta.

While Zio spoke with the old man, the sheep drifted toward our stopped car and surrounded it on both sides, their little faces barely reaching up to the bottom of our car windows, *baaing* all the while. Our car was like a pebble in a stream that causes the water to part as it cascades down against the current; our car was playing the role of the pebble, and those beautiful white animals seemed to be cascading past us.

It could have been a scene from a black-and-white Fellini movie. I would love to have photos or a video of it, but who brings a camera to Cheese Day? Not me. At least not this day. Not even a phone that could have stood in as a camera; I wasn't expecting any calls on Cheese Day, you know. So, I need to rely on the video camera in my head to replay that surreal and lovely scene; hopefully the video won't get weathered and washed out with age – my age, that is.

But retelling the story helps to keep it fresh. So, after Zio got the directions, the shepherd again directed the sheep away from our car with his well-choreographed routine of staff and dogs ... staff and dogs ... staff and dogs ... until we were able to pull away and cruise on into the village of Pietraroja, an oddly named village in Italy, I always thought, its spelling seeming to be more Spanish than Italian, but it's one with a great history nonetheless. It was originally settled by the Samnites and is famous for the fact that a fossil of a baby dinosaur was discovered there, the first such discovery in Italy.

Once inside the village, we easily found the Bellos' nicely appointed home, which had a cool, stone side room downstairs where Laura made and stored that precious pecorino. And while Dad was quite deliberately and studiously selecting the rounds of cheese that would accompany us home to America, who should amble into the room ... but the shepherd himself! He was none other than Angelo Bello's father and had known all along that we were the "Americans" who were coming to his son's home to buy up that pecorino. He told us that the sheep we had passed in our Fiat were the very ones that produced the milk for the cheese we were in the process of buying.

We all pulled up small wooden chairs with wicker seats and arranged them in a circle so we could share a few glasses of wine, homemade naturally, along with some hunks of that sharp, fresh cheese and more than a few laughs and stories.

Yes, it would have been nice to have a camera to record that scene, too, but it doesn't matter, after all: I'll never forget it.

10

A' Salute!

Amici e vini sono meglio vecchi. – *Old Italian proverb*

Literally: Friends and wines are better when they are old *(or improve with age.)*

Questa è la terra della temperanza, quando tengo u bicchiere di vino dentr'a panza. – *Proverb in the Neapolitan dialect*

Literally: This is a great land when you've got a glass of wine in your belly. *(The implication being it's not so great when you don't. A humorous rhyming proverb for when you are sitting around drinking wine.)*

When my former brother-in-law was courting my sister Lisa and would stop over to the house, my father would always offer him wine – whether it was the homemade red that Dad has made faithfully every year since coming to the United States, or whether it was what he used to call the "store-bought" stuff.

It didn't matter which because either way, Dwayne always politely declined. Growing up with an Irish and Scandinavian heritage, wine usually was not something that was on his agenda – or his table.

However, he did enjoy a beer or whiskey every now and again. One evening when he stopped by, Dad and a buddy were drinking grappa along with their vino. When Dwayne asked what the clear liquor was, Dad explained to him that grappa was sort of like whiskey made from grape pressings, figuring that might capture Dwayne's fancy.

To capture that fancy even more, Dad thought he would show off the exciting nature of grappa. He poured a splash of it down the center of the kitchen table and lit it with a lighter. A spectacular blue streak of flame immediately shot down the table as Dad – no scientist, but that's OK – told us that the blue in the flame showed that the alcohol was pure, the best kind.

Did I mention that this was homemade grappa, too, by the way?

Also, did I mention that Dad did not realize it, but he had spilled a few drops of it on his thumb, and while he was regaling Dwayne with grappa talk, he didn't notice that his thumb also was ablaze, the flame so high that it almost singed his eyebrows?

Dwayne shrieked in horror. Dad quickly extinguished his thumb. Everyone had a good laugh.

And Dwayne said, with a dramatic pause suitable for Shakespeare, "Uh, I think I'll try … the wine."

Ironically, he liked that wine so much once he tasted it, we couldn't get him to stop drinking the stuff (or maybe he was just afraid that another pyrogenic show might be in the offing if we didn't stick to wine). We called ourselves *La Squadra di Vino*, which loosely translates to The Wine Team, and we gathered quite often to raise a few glasses. We even had golf shirts with *Squadra di Vino* embroidered on the breast.

Vino is a big part of our life, just as it is of many families' lives in the Old Country. My grandfather, like most farmers in southern Italy, grew grapes along with the rest of his vegetables. He sold some to commercial wineries, and he kept some for himself that he then made into wine for the family.

I still remember the first time I ever saw his wine cellar, which had been dug out by hand at the rear of his farm house. My Dad made his wine in two 50-gallon oak barrels at home, and I thought *that* was a lot. My grandfather had a half-dozen or so 50-gallon barrels and another five or six of what must have been 100-gallon monsters. He also had a press that seemed like the size of Delaware, so large that it had to be turned by horses or mules to squeeze out that precious wine.

I guess what I'm trying to say is that it was some serious amount of wine that he made for the family.

I also don't want to come off sounding like all Italians are winos and heavy drinkers. Wine is not the only thing that they consume – obviously, there's a lot of macaroni and bread and prosciutto and provolone cheese and apricots and tomatoes. But wine really is a major player on nearly every table along with all those great foods.

Dad makes red and white versions and in recent years has even turned out a nice sparkling wine, even though he doesn't really prefer it. He knows how good it is, though, and how much others like it, which is why he makes it. He uses California grapes, which he says are most similar to those grown in Italy. He makes it in the fall and starts drinking it when it's way too young – primarily because he can't wait for it to age. And it's gone long before it should be, sometimes around Easter! In those cases, he has to drink the "store-bought" stuff until he makes another batch the next fall.

Tradition with Dad is that almost every time we empty a bottle, he'll pick it up by the neck, look at the bottom of it, shake his head sadly, and say, "This one must have had a hole in the bottom. All the wine leaked out."

Sometimes he'll add to the patter by saying, "You know, these guys can make a pretty good wine, but they can't make a good bottle."

And no matter what time of day or night it is or how many glasses of vino he's had that day, whenever someone new comes to the table and lifts a glass for the first time, he'll say, in a toast: "First one today."

In 2001, in a personal effort to keep the wine making tradition going, and also to be able to use Dad as a consultant while he was still going strong, a few of my buddies and I bought some equipment – a grinder, a press, some oak barrels, some glass carboys – combined forces and began making our own red wine.

Even though we live in the Finger Lakes Region, upstate New York's ultimate grape-growing zone, we also bought California grapes to best duplicate Dad's recipe. We were only able to get Zinfandel grapes that first year, but we also bought Cabernet juice to mix with them, our own idea of what we thought would be a nice blend for a table wine.

Consulting Dad every step of the way, we grinded the grapes – stems and all – tossed them in a big blue plastic barrel with the juice and let it all ferment together for a few days, continually pushing the bubbling-up liquid down with a pitchfork (Dad uses a broom handle ... oh well, the pitchfork represented modern progress, I suppose).

When it was ready, we pressed the skins and pulp to get more super-concentrated juice out of them. We put all our wine in two 50-gallon French oak barrels in the basement of one of my *paisani*. We racked it off a couple of times, which is sort of like filtering it without a filter. That is, we would carefully siphon the wine out of one container, leaving any sediment behind, and put it into a new container, usually a glass carboy. A word of caution, though, you never want to rack your wine when the moon is full, at least according to my father who warns that if you do, it remains cloudy (the wine that is, not the moon). We made our own labels, calling our first vintage "*Il Padrino,*" The Godfather of all our wines, and later we bottled it all up.

I probably can be accused of being a bit biased, but our first vino tasted pretty good. We learned that we didn't want to grind the stems up along with everything else, so in subsequent vintages when using grapes, we would pull the fruit from the stems. However, it didn't hurt that first batch too much. I have been making vino ever since. Some vintages are better than others, but the nice thing about it is every time I lift a glass to my lips, I'm not just drinking homemade wine, but I'm honoring my dad and my *nonno* and the rest of my ancestors who went through the very same process, mindful, of course, of full moons.

A' salute! To your health!

11

Soccer: From the 'Cavaliere' to Watering the Tomatoes

"Chiunque abbia inventato il calcio dovrebbe essere adorato come un Dio."
  – Anonymous

Literally: Whoever invented soccer should be celebrated like a God.

No collection of stories about Italy and Italians is complete without a few words – or a few thousand – about their favorite sport. Soccer, to us; *calcio*, to them, which comes from the verb *calciare*, to kick.

It's a simple game: A ball, two goals and 22 players. It is said to have the fewest rules of any major sport – called the 17 Laws of Soccer. Simple or complicated, it doesn't matter; either way it is revered in Italy like a religion.

During the worldwide gasoline crunch in the 1970s, the Italian government joined many others around the world in passing gas-saving regulations including prohibiting all private cars and trucks from being on the roads on Sundays; all that were allowed were emergency vehicles, large people-movers such as buses, and taxis.

Sounded good … in theory.

In Italy, Sundays – besides being reserved for going to Mass and eating *mamma's* macaroni – are soccer days, just as they are for pro football in America. However, even with the strictly-enforced edict, attendance, apparently, did not seem to drop off at all those soccer games. Officials were puzzled at first, though they did notice that there were thousands upon thousands of yellow taxis parked around the various stadiums throughout the country on game days. It didn't take much of an investigation to reveal what was happening – fans were painting their own personal cars to look like taxis so they could drive to the games!

Yes, it seems, every Tom, Dick and Giovanni suddenly had a taxi cab in the family fleet.

My Dad, himself a lifelong player, coach and fan, told me that story once to point out the fanaticism with which Italians follow *calcio*. I've never been able to verify it, but somehow, I believe it probably is true. And if it isn't, as someone wise once said, it ought to be.

Dad also told me about a particular stadium that was despised by referees because the soccer fans in the town were notoriously poor losers. They were known to storm the field after – and sometimes during – games to let the referees know their displeasure with certain calls.

It got so bad that club officials put barbed-wire fencing up around the field and then dug a moat around that to keep the fans at bay. Undeterred, an angry – and somewhat industrious, it must be said – mob would rip up the wooden bleachers and lay the planks over the fence and across the moat so they could climb their way onto the field!

In another step, officials decided bolting those wooden planks down would be more prudent, but again, those ever-resourceful fans smuggled wrenches into the stadium, loosened the bolts and again used the planks to gain access to the field and those dastardly referees.

As a final resort, the soccer club paid for a helicopter to be lowered onto the field as soon as the final whistle blew after a heated game to pick up unpopular referees and carry them off to safety. No word on what might have happened if the helicopter pilot happened to be a fan of the home team.

Again, I didn't run that one through Snopes to see if it is true, but it certainly wouldn't surprise me.

We hear every now and again about riots among soccer fans in Europe, and indeed around the world, and we might think, "Who are those crazy people, getting all worked up over a soccer game?" But many of us just don't have any idea of the passion they have for the game, even misguided as it is, at times. Remember, too, that while in America there are four major professional sports – baseball, football, basketball and hockey – and numerous semi-major ones, in Italy, there is only soccer at the top of the mountain with Formula One auto racing, competitive cycling and maybe volleyball competing for a few other fans.

My Dad loved *calcio* from an early age, but the son of farmers in the small village of San Salvatore Telesino, he was needed in his parents' fields, not on the village's soccer pitch. The allure was too strong, though, especially as he matured into a strong young man and one of the most gifted players in town. He concocted a scheme that got him out of the house every Sunday so that he could play ball with the local squad.

He would dress in a nice suit, complete with tie, as was the fashion of the day, and tell his mother and father that he was waiting for his cousin Salvatore, and together they were going out to meet some pretty young girls in the village *piazza* to maybe have some *gelato* and then possibly go dancing. His parents were thrilled about the idea because it was about time for young *Michele* to meet some nice girls. In the meantime, Dad would pack his soccer gear into a small duffle bag and when Salvatore pulled up in the alley in the back of their house on his motor scooter and honked the horn, Dad would toss that bag down to him from his second-story bedroom window. He'd then bounce down the stairs, kiss his mother goodbye, bound out the door and climb on the back of Salvatore's scooter. Off to the game ... er, to the pretty girls they would go.

Dad would change into his soccer uniform, play in the game, accept the accolades from the fans who enjoyed watching him play, then change back into his dress clothes for the return trip home.

This worked like a charm for many, many weeks – or at least Dad thought. Stories of his exploits on the soccer pitch made their way around that small village. Also, cousins, aunts and uncles were in the crowds that watched him play, and they simply were unable to keep their feelings bottled up. They gushed about *Michele*, who was nicknamed "*Il Cavaliere*" – or the "gentlemanly" – player. Eventually, unbeknown to Dad, the reviews made their way to his *mamma* and *papà* who allowed him to continue the well-worked scheme for a few more weeks and a

*The group that played in the **amichevole** on Sardinia in which Dad was named Mario Ranieri. He is in the center, just over the guy who is lounging.*

few more big games until one Sunday, as he returned from the field and bounded up the stairs toward his room, he was stopped in his tracks when his *mamma* called out, "Who won the game today, Michele?"

"What?" Dad asked sheepishly. "You knew all along?"

"Well, not all along," his father said, "but when we kept hearing about this 'Cavaliere ... the Great Cavaliere' we had to find out who that was, don't you think?"

Busted and red-faced, Dad went upstairs to his room. His parents, as much as they needed him in the fields, allowed him to finish out that season and help bring San Salvatore Telesino a regional championship.

Dad dreamed of playing for big-time professional teams. And though it was rare for those clubs to scout players in the poor south, a few did come calling. However, when they did, his mother nixed those dreams.

"The ball won't put food on your table," Dad remembers her saying. Often.

If only she were alive today to see the multimillion-dollar contracts that professional soccer players in Italy can command! I have a feeling she would feel differently about the whole "food on the table" thing.

Dad also loves telling the story about when he was "recruited" to play for a police academy squad. He was about 18 years old and was doing his required military duty as a radio operator for the Italian Army in Cagliari on the island of Sardinia. Dad's commander was friends with the head of the nearby police academy, and when that friend lined up an *amichevole* – or "friendly" match – against a team of Air Force academy cadets, he asked the commander if he could recommend a couple of good players from among his young soldiers. The commander volunteered Dad and another man to play with the police cadets.

The only problem was that Dad couldn't play under his real name, because he was not registered in the police academy. He would have to play under the name of a man who actually attended the academy. They chose to call him Mario Ranieri.

Dad – or Mario – acquitted himself quite nicely, and even scored a goal in the match as the police academy cadets pulled off a beautifully played 2-0 win (ironically, the other goal was scored by the other player recommended by the commander).

After the match there was a lovely banquet for both teams with a gorgeous spread of food and wine. The Police cadets and the Air Force cadets all dressed in their sharpest uniforms and there was an "inspection" of the players before dinner. The chief of police came to look over the academy cadets and to offer his congratulations on a game well played. When he got do Dad in the line, he stopped and complimented him on his goal and how elegantly he carried himself on the field. "What's your name, cadet?" he asked, and Dad recalls that as he started to say "Michele Cutillo," the head of the academy who had recruited him blurted out "Mario Ranieri ... That's Mario Ranieri, sir!"

Dad caught himself, recognizing what was happening, saluted and said, "Yessir, that's right. I am Mario Ranieri, sir."

The police chief said, "Well, Mario, you are a damn fine player, and you are going to make a damn fine police officer! Fantastic job, Mario Ranieri. The police academy is proud to have young men like you among our ranks."

Dad just smiled and nodded at the chief, figuring the less he said at that point, the better.

But that is how he became known as Mario Ranieri – at least for one fleeting-yet-memorable day – and is a sampling of the passion Italians have for *calcio*. Sunday dinners are planned around watching games on TV, listening to them on the radio or going to see them in person, whether in your regular car or one painted to look like a taxi.

I was in Italy in 1990 when FIFA's World Cup tournament was being played there, and it was amazing to see the enthusiasm and fervor the entire country had for the sport's world championship event, which – like the Olympics – is contested every four years and pits the best teams on the planet against each other. The intervening three years are spent attempting to qualify for the 32 final spots, and every country in the world, from A-Z – literally, from Afghanistan to Zimbabwe – gives it a shot.

I have been fortunate enough to attend four World Cup tournaments with my Dad, including the 2006 tournament which was held in Germany. Dad, my buddy Kevin Hulslander and I went to both semifinal games that year, including Italy's monumental 2-0 upset of Germany in Dortmund; in the other semifinal France beat Portugal 1-0 in Munich. By the time the championship match was played in Berlin, we had made our way to Italy so we watched the Italians claim the world title with an exciting win over France. We were in the small Tuscan town of Castellina in Chianti at the time and enjoyed the game on a big-screen TV set up outside at a local café; then we watched the locals in that small town party and parade up and down the streets from deep into the night until early the next morning after Italy had won.

In 1998, we were in France, and we went to a quarterfinal game in Paris in which the French took on Italy. It was the first time I had ever seen Italy play live and in person, though in a stadium that held 80,000 people there were probably only 5,000 or so rooting for Italy – if that!

After a scoreless regulation and overtime, the French went on to win in a heartbreaking penalty-kick shootout.

We were surrounded by French fans in the stands who knew we were rooting for the Italians, especially my father. And as nasty as we know opposing fans can be, we certainly did not experience it that day from the folks around us. As a little tear rolled down my Dad's cheek after the game, they consoled him in the gentlest and most heart-warming fashion, patting him on the back and telling him that Italy had put up a strong fight. My Dad returned the favor by telling them he was going to be rooting for their France to win the championship from that point on, which they did.

As we were walking out of the stadium, an Italian television reporter spotted Dad's Italian baseball cap and asked if he could interview him. Dad consented, and they spoke, in Italian, about the game for a bit and the crushing defeat. Then the reporter said to Dad, "That's a difficult game to watch, considering you came hundreds of miles from Italy to watch it, no?"

My Dad replied, "What *hundreds* of miles? I came from *thousands* of miles to watch this game. I'm from the United States!"

The reporter was even more flabbergasted.

Italy is one of only three countries to win four World Cup championships or more and was all kinds of decked out to host that 1990 Cup. Dusty, centuries-old towns and villages, whose normal colors are gray and brown, were decorated with green, white and red banners, flags and ribbons. World Cup posters adorned café and restaurant windows. Everyone, it seemed, on the entire peninsula and onto the islands of Sicily and Sardinia – from bus drivers to *carabinieri* to 80-year-old *nonnas* as they boiled water for rigatoni – was talking about Italy's chances to win "*Il Mondiale.*"

The home country's national team, known as the "*Azzurri,*" or the Blues because of their uniform jersey color, was an enchanting collection of players that year, and the country's passionate fans celebrated each victory through the early stages of the tournament with increasing zeal. However, the cheering came to a screeching halt when Italy was upset in the semifinals by Argentina, again in the cruelest of fashions via *another* penalty kick shootout, a contrived one-on-one crapshoot used to determine a winner after a game is tied through regulation and overtime.

I watched the game on television with my uncle, *Zio Enzo*, a retired general in the Italian Army, along with my Dad. It started late in the evening, and so it was nearly midnight by the time it was over, and Italy had been dealt that harsh and crushing blow. As the Argentines celebrated on the TV screen in front of us, I turned to check out my uncle's reaction, but he was nowhere to be found.

He was out in his yard. Under a full moon. Watering his tomatoes.

I wanted to console him, but Dad told me it was better just to leave him be. He said that Zio Enzo needed some time to himself, some time to unwind, some time to collect his thoughts.

He watered those *pomodori* for about an hour, and when he came back inside, his eyes were as red as the tomatoes.

It was such a perfect metaphor to me: Water trickling out of the hose and onto the receptive tomatoes, while tears were trickling down my uncle's cheeks.

The next day, the sun – naturally – rose again. But it didn't seem to burn as bright in the blue Italian sky. The wine was still poured, but it didn't seem to have the same zing. The food was still abundant and fresh (especially the tomatoes), but it seemed just a little flat. We read about a railroad conductor whose train was about 10 minutes from the station in Rome when the result of the game was announced. He stopped the train to cry for about 15 minutes before proceeding on into the station.

Just a soccer game? Not quite.

12

Baseball, Apple Pie and... Linguine?

Non è finita finché è finita. – *Famous saying by Italian-American Hall of Fame ballplayer Yogi Berra translated into Italian*

Literally: It ain't over till it's over.

Dad loves baseball.

Not in the traditional sense of a man who can wax poetic for hours about the beauty of a well-executed hit-and-run play, who nostalgically laments the fact that no one can bunt anymore, or who can tell you why it was anti-American for both the Brooklyn Dodgers and the New York Giants to move to the West Coast in 1957.

No, my Dad loves it because when he goes to a ballgame, he can catch up on his sleep.

There is no better place to catch a few winks than in a ballpark's highest bleacher seats on a lazy sunny afternoon with maybe a warm summer breeze gently caressing you, your cap pulled down over your eyes, your hands crossed behind your head.

Just ask him.

Who needs Ny-Quil? If Dad has trouble dozing off, he can turn on a Padres-Cubs game and be out before the umpire hollers "Play Ball!"

Although, truth be told, Dad could fall asleep in the front row of a Rolling Stones concert, too, but that's another whole story. This one is about America's pastime and an attempt by an Italian father of American children to try to appreciate baseball, a sport he never saw, heard of, played or even knew existed before he came to the United States in 1958.

America may be home to baseball, apple pie and Chevrolet, but in his homeland, it's more like soccer, linguine with marinara sauce and Fiat. Totally different lifestyles, of course, but Dad did his best to do what was right by his young American son.

The biggest problem, though, was that he didn't understand a lick of the game. He still doesn't, really, after all these years. That can make it boring. If you don't know what I mean, try watching cricket, and if you have any idea what the heck is happening between those wickets, please let me know. I had a British friend who couldn't understand why American sports fans thought soccer was so boring because it was low scoring. He used to say, "We've got a game in England that's the highest scoring bloody game of all-time, where hundreds and hundreds of runs can be scored; and sometimes the games last for days. If you want offense, you've got it. It's called cricket, and it's the most … bloody … boring … sport in the history of mankind."

But I digress.

Dad tried with the baseball thing. Boy, did he try, but he just didn't get it. If you want a comedy routine you should see him explaining the game, in his words, to his friends and family in the Old Country, who also don't understand it and are used to a game like soccer that flows for the entire time with very few breaks in the action.

We're at Dad's friend Antonio's house with about 30 people sitting around the table. All eyes are on Dad as he sets the scene, like an Italian version of Bob Costas:

"OK, the pitcher, he's ready … and the batter, he's ready, too. And that pitcher, he gets that ball and he throws that pitch, and OK, we've finally got some action going … and the batter … lets it go. Nothing."

"Ball one!!"

His audience breaks up with laughter, but Costas … er, Dad, gets them all wound up again.

"OK, well, the pitcher, he's ready again, and everyone is waiting for some really good action this time, and that pitcher, he gets that ball and here he goes again, and he throws that ball in to the batter … and … and … nothing happens."

"Ball two!"

More roars of laughter by the assembled fans.

"Well, it doesn't matter because now it is really getting exciting, believe me, even though we're still waiting for some action. But that's OK because this pitcher and this batter, they are really, really ready now alright. And that pitcher takes the ball and he throws a fast one, really fast … and the batter … he … he … watches it go by."

"Strike one!"

More howls. And this, Dad assures his audience, goes on for hours … and hours. Sort of about the length of time it takes him to lay out that play by play at Antonio's table.

Speaking of play by play, the first time Dad ever took me to a pro baseball game in Syracuse, New York, I remember the score was tied in the bottom of the ninth and the hometown Chiefs – a minor-league affiliate of the famous New York Yankees at the time – were battling, trying to pull out a win. Dad turned to me, his young American son who was squeezing for a big hit, and said, "Don't you worry, son, this guy will SCORE a home run."

I rolled my eyes incredulously and said, "Dad, no, they HIT a home run, they don't SCORE a home run. They score a RUN. Sheesh, don't you know anything?"

Now, this was a man who called it a HIT even when the batter made an OUT. Can you believe that craziness? The batter would ground one to the shortstop who would throw him out easily at first base, and Dad would say, "Wow, now that's a nice HIT right there."

"No, Dad, that is not a HIT, that's an OUT," I corrected.

"But he HIT it. Why isn't it a HIT?" Dad would ask. I guess the question was logical in a Yogi Berra sort of way. It also was an impossible question for a 9-year-old to answer in any sensible way.

"Because it's not a HIT, it's an OUT," I answered, sort of in the way Mom used to answer my "Why?" when I was questioning her authority – "Because I said so, that's why."

Of course, next thing you knew, a batter would slug a home run and some nearby fan would cheer, "Way to HIT it OUT, buddy."

And Dad would go, "That's not an OUT, that's a HIT."

And the guy would say, "That's not what I said; I said way to HIT it OUT."

Did you ever get a headache watching baseball? It seemed like every time we went to a ball game, an Abbott and Costello routine would break out.

Anyway, back to the bottom of the ninth and Rusty Torres, the Chiefs' fan favorite, who naturally – exactly as per Dad's prediction – belted a game-winning home run to the delight of all his fans, young and old. And that's also precisely when I knew my Dad was magic, no matter how he spoke or that he didn't know the difference between hits and outs.

"See, I told you there was nothing to worry about. I told you that guy would SCORE a home run," Dad said proudly as we walked out of the stadium, hand in hand.

"Yup, Dad, you were right. He did SCORE a home run."

Speaking of scoring – or rather, hitting – home runs, Mike Piazza belted 427 of them in a spectacular Major League career that would lead to his induction into the National Baseball Hall of Fame in Cooperstown, New York.

By its very nature, the Hall of Fame, like all museums, is a treasure trove of history, memorabilia and collections, a magical place where answers to untold trivia questions can be found.

In 2016, at the annual Hall of Fame Induction Ceremony on July 24 – with Piazza at the podium – it also became the home to the answer of a brand-new question:

What famous baseball player, during his Hall of Fame induction speech, proudly spoke a sentence in Italian for the entire sporting world to hear?

If you answered Mike Piazza, go to the head of the class.

Piazza, a robust, slugging catcher who played primarily for two teams, the Los Angeles Dodgers and the New York Mets, was one of two greats enshrined in the Hall that day — the other being Ken Griffey Jr.

Piazza was making his speech to about 52,000 sun-drenched fans

— said to be the second-largest Induction Day crowd in Cooperstown history — when he mentioned his dad.

"My father, Vince, was the son of Italian immigrants. He's so proud of his Italian heritage ..."

Then he uttered the phrase that will be part of the answer to that trivia question: *Un grazie infinito al paese Italia che ha fatto il regalo di mio padre.*

Translation: A big thank you to the country of Italy that produced the gift of my father.

His father, who had suffered a major stroke a couple of years earlier, looked up at his son from that crowd with tears in his eyes, and Piazza – the big, strong, Hall of Fame catcher – choked up as he went on to talk about Vince, and his mother, Veronica, whom, he said, "gave me the greatest gift a mother can give a child ... she gave me the gift of my Catholic faith."

It was a touching moment that had nothing to do with baseball, yet it was baseball that provided this stage and proved once again how much Italians and Italian-Americans have contributed to the fabric of America, even to its national pastime. They are men with names like Yogi Berra, Roy Campanella, Joe DiMaggio, Tommy Lasorda, Tony Lazzeri, Phil Rizzuto, Tony LaRussa, Joe Torre, Ron Santo. All Hall of Famers; in short, some of the greatest the game has ever produced.

And as Piazza took his place among those all-time greats, he may have been the proudest of all them about his Italian ancestry. He travels to Italy often and at the time was looking to put his three young children in an Italian school for a year or two. He even bought a majority ownership in a professional soccer team, A.C. Reggiana 1919.

"I've been going to Italy since 2006, the first time I played for Italy in the [World Baseball] Classic and just fell in love with soccer," Piazza explained at a press conference the day before the Induction Ceremony. "I looked at a couple of business opportunities and just decided to jump in the water and give it a shot and really experience what it's like to be a club owner, to run the business."

Piazza owned about 60 percent of the team, which finished seventh in 2016 in one of Italy's minor leagues and made the second round of the Italian Cup. It is in Reggio Emilia, a city of about 170,000 people in northern Italy between Bologna and Parma.

"It's a beautiful city and extremely passionate," Piazza said. "The food is some of the most spectacular in Italy. Those teams over there, you have to work on them, you have to be smart and have discipline. I'm excited to do it. I don't know where it will lead. All I know is it's been a lot of fun and we'll see where it goes."

It was an interesting juxtaposition, I thought, the grandson of Italian immigrants who made a name for himself shining in America's national sport going back to his roots and attempting to make a name for himself in Italy's national sport.

Sadly, it did not go all that well for the Hall of Famer. By the summer of 2018, the 100-year-old soccer club was officially bankrupt and Piazza and his wife, whom he had turned ownership of the club over to a year earlier, were basically run out of town. The mayor of the town said the Piazzas "disrespected" the city and there were death threats painted on the club's headquarters.

It's sort of like Dad was trying to say when he did the funny play-by-play routine at Antonio's table: Maybe baseball and Italy don't quite go hand in hand.

13

History Lessons
Abound in bell'Italia

Tutte le strade conducono a Roma. – *Old Italian proverb*
Literally: All roads lead to Rome.

I am a history buff, and as much as I enjoy learning and reading about America's past, unless you are studying the Native Americans, that history goes back only about 400 years or so, to when the Pilgrims arrived on the Mayflower.

In Italy, the narrative goes back 2,000 years. Or more. And that is living history, by the way, of people, of towns, of the land, of wars. Think about that for a second: 2,000 years … and still going strong. In fact, there is one city in the southern region of Basilicata near the Adriatic Sea called Matera, a UNESCO World Heritage site, that is said to be one of the three oldest continually inhabited cities in the history of the world, dating back to 15,000 BC.

One of my best friends, Ken Boyd, came to Italy with me in 1990. Another fan of history, Ken kept touching buildings and statues in and around Dad's village and saying, "This is the oldest thing I've ever touched." He did it wherever we went, feeling that ancient history in a palpable, tactile way. Eventually, we went to Rome and visited the Flavian Amphitheatre – better known to you and me as the Colosseum. Ken's eyes lit up, and I knew what was coming next. Started in 72 AD under the emperor Vespasian, the Colosseum was completed eight years later in 80. When Ken got to lay his paw on it, it was 1,910 years old.

Some busts that were found in San Salvatore Telesino on display in the Abbey.

"OK, now this? *This* is old," Ken said. "I don't need to touch anything else."

We never made it to Matera on that trip, but if we had, Ken would have had a field day.

As much as I enjoy learning about Italy's incredibly fascinating history, that reading has mostly been about the major peoples and areas – those Romans, the powerful Venetians, Florence and the Renaissance, the Popes, Naples, Sicily's incredible story. Somewhat amazingly I never really delved into the history of my father's small town of San Salvatore Telesino.

Of course, my grandparents came from there, and Dad and my uncle, and dozens and dozens of cousins, but other than family, I didn't really know its history.

I guess I really didn't think it had that much history, but in Italy *everyplace* has history. And a story.

On a September 2016 trip back to visit family with my Dad, I really struck it rich. There is an old Benedictine abbey in San Salvatore Telesino that over the decades had fallen into disrepair. I'd always wanted to visit it, but on most of my other visits, I usually found it closed. However, a 2010 project not only restored it magnificently but also transformed it into something of a museum of the village. I happened to come across it on a beautifully sunny Sunday afternoon when it was open, so I popped in and even managed to get a young woman to give me a private tour.

Now, San Salvatore Telesino – in the province of Benevento and about 30 miles northeast of Naples – is no major tourist destination whatsoever. It's not even a *minor* tourist destination, in all honesty. It's a small farming village of about 4,000 people in the hills between Caserta and Benevento, known as the *Valle Telesina*. When I am there – this visitor from America – I definitely can feel the eyes of the natives upon me.

OK, surely, I was a stranger in their town but unlike Rome and Naples and Venice and all the other grand cities that are packed with strangers, San Salvatore Telesino doesn't get too many of them. There really isn't anything to draw the strangers – or tourists – there. Or is there?

What I found out that day astonished me, though perhaps it shouldn't have.

San Salvatore Telesino goes back to at least 300 B.C. Rome is only about 450 years older, Venice only about 100 years older. And Florence is about 250 years *younger*. I had to process that one for a second – the magnificent and historic city of Florence hadn't been around as long as San Salvatore Telesino. Hmmmm.

Dad's village was, at first, an ancient Samnite city and later became a Roman colony. The Samnites were an Italic people who at times were at war with Rome and at other times were in accord with the Republic. Perhaps their most famous citizen was Pontius Pilate, the man best known for his role in the trial and crucifixion of Jesus and a man whose name comes up during every single Roman Catholic Mass when the Apostles' Creed is recited.

Roman dictator Lucius Cornelius Sulla oversaw an ethnic cleansing of the Samnites that wiped them out about 80 BC. With the Sam-

The centuries-old Benedictine Abbey in San Salvatore Telesino.

nites disposed of, the area including Dad's village came under the rule of Rome. There was a statue in the town dedicated to Tiberius Iulius Caesar Nero Gemellus, who was the adopted son of Augustus Caesar and a cousin to future Roman ruler Caligula. I don't know what he did in or for that small village, but to think that one of the Caesars had a connection to San Salvatore Telesino amazed me. That's some history, alright.

By the way, Saint Salvatore, for whom the village is named, was born in Spain but spent the final years of his life on the Italian island of Sardinia. The Benedictine abbey in Dad's town, built in the 10th century, was dedicated to him and to St. Anselm, who is said to have excavated a well at the abbey that I was able to visit on my guided tour.

It is said that the abbey was built using the Norman style of architecture, which also is known as Romanesque and character-ized by semi-circular arches. The first known abbot of it was Leopol-do, who was first mentioned in historical writings in 1075. I wouldn't know Leopoldo from Leo the Lion, but I do know – thanks to my buddy Ken – that 1075 was one heck of a long time ago. In 1098, just a few years later, under the abbot Giovanni, the monastery hosted Saint Anselm of Aosta who had held the position of archbishop of Canterbury from 1093 to 1109 and in addition to being a terrific well excavator was also a philosopher, theologian, and prolific writer. The Oxford Dictionary of the Christian Church says that Anselm has been called "the most luminous and penetrating intellect between St. Augustine and St. Thomas Aquinas" and "the father of scholasticism," a method of critical thought. So, he had that going for him, besides being able to excavate a pretty solid-looking well. Again, like Caesar, to think that this acclaimed human being, canonized as a saint after his death in 1109, perhaps took long, pensive walks on land where Dad kicked his soccer ball around just boggles my mind.

That abbey, in addition to frescoes – including one dated about 1300 – other artwork, and pieces of statues on display also had two large modern-day photographs that showed ruins of a small Roman amphitheater and of Roman city walls that still exist in San Salvatore Telesino.

Here is the most incredible part of this story – those ruins are on land that used to belong to my grandfather and great-grandfather. In fact, the little farm house in which my father was born, is right next to the ruins of that amphitheater. Sadly, they usually are overrun by wild growth, and it is too costly for Dad's small village to maintain the site regularly. However, every now and again those ruins are cleaned up when an influx of money – whether from the government or a private donor – flows into the village coffers. I have been able to visit the ruins in both conditions, cleaned up and overrun. Nothing like the Roman Colosseum, of course, but they are historic and exquisitely interesting in their own right.

So, there you have it, one of the places I most overlooked and least expected to have such a wealth of history was literally right in my dad's backyard.

I encourage you all to research and learn about the famous land of your forefathers. You just never know what you might turn up.

Christmas Eves past, like this one from 1989, always included Dad dressing up with a flashing bowtie and some sort of holiday-appropriate hat, like this reindeer model.

Me as a child, standing by a Christmas tree.

14

'Natale,'
A Great Time to be Italian

Natale con i tuoi e Pasqua con chi vuoi – *Old Italian proverb*

Christmas with your family and Easter with whomever you want
*(in other words, you must spend Christmas with your family, while Easter
can be spent with anyone!)*

It's Christmas at our house, the door is open wide ...
It's Christmas at our house, don't knock ... just come inside.

Those are some of the words to one of the greatest Christmas songs you never heard of, "Christmas At Our House," recorded on a 1992 album by New Jersey-born, Italian-American crooner Lou Monte, who you may know better for another slightly more famous song, "Dominick the Donkey." Ee-aw, ee-aw!

But with apologies to the famous – and getting more famous with each passing year – *ciuccio (chooch,)* the words from "Christmas At Our House" really struck a chord in our family as we grew up. First, Lou Monte was as much a staple in our record player as Dean Martin, Sinatra and Tony Bennett. After all, Lou also gave us "Pepino the Italian Mouse," not quite as famous as Dominick but a funny rascal, nonetheless (And kids, if you don't know what a record player is, ask your parents!)

More importantly, though, that door-wide-open thing, that don't-knock-just-come-in thing, that's what our parents' home was like back in the day, especially at Christmastime. I'll bet a lot of yours were like that, too. It was one of the great things about growing up Italian-American.

My father gets ready to open a special bottle of homemade vino for Christmas.

I know we've all seen those lists and YouTube videos on the internet about growing up Italian or "You know you're Italian when ..." but to me, nothing rang truer than the holiday that celebrated the birth of Christ. It was – and is – the best time ever to be Napoletano ... or Siciliano ... or Calabrese ... or Milanese ... or Abruzzese ... or ... well, you get the picture.

No book about growing up Italian or Italian-American is complete without at least one chapter on the Christmas holiday, *Natale*. The word literally means birthplace in Italian, and when used in the holiday context it is referring to the birth of Jesus.

So, here is what celebrating *Natale* meant to me along with some of the memories that I have from holidays past:

• Speaking Italian – As you read in earlier chapters, it usually was more important for Dad to speak English around the house instead of Italian. There was one very large exception to that house rule, however – Christmastime. Mom didn't speak much Italian, only a little of the San Salvatorese dialect, but around the holidays, the two of them seemed to converse much more frequently in some sort of language that their young children did not understand – imagine that! I can't tell you what they were saying, but I can tell you that every year, Santa managed to somehow deliver exactly what we kids were looking for.

• Homemade wine – Something else that we've examined in earlier chapters. Dad loved some of Italy's best wines, most notably Chianti and Valpolicella from up north, but his hands-down favorite, especially around the holidays, was his own homemade red. The celebrations in our parents' house were always kicked up a notch or two after the homemade vino had been flowing for a while and the cheeks got rosier.

• Seafood – Of course, as tradition holds, Christmas Eve in Catholic households is for seafood. It held for many, many years at Mom and Dad's house where they and Uncle Louie would cook up everything for the feast, including linguine with clams, fried smelt, broccoli and shrimp, baccalà, mussels, baked haddock and something that is Dad's own concoction that he calls "meatless meatballs" – that is, everything that is in meatballs … except the meat – which you also have read about in a previous chapter. As the years went on, Dad sort of relented in the face of the protests from his American relatives who insisted that meat should be included at the feast, so in later celebrations he also did a roast with pan-baked potatoes, ham, regular meatballs, braciole and homemade sausage and a bunch of other meat dishes for the "Merigans." Holding on to his personal tradition, though, Dad would not eat any of the meat … until after midnight. At 12:01 – while some of the family would be out at Midnight Mass – he would load up a big plate with slices of roast beef, some meatballs, ham, and any other meat, stick it in the microwave and go to town.

• Singing – No holiday party in our family was complete without dad breaking into song, complete with his battery-operated, red, flashing bow-tie and his baseball cap with reindeer antlers. The favorites over the years boiled down to a precious handful – Dean Martin's "That's Amore," Lou Monte's "Pepino," "Dominick" and "Christmas At Our House," Adriano Celentano's "Azzurro," and Julius LaRosa's "Eh Cumpari!" Actually, I guess those last two didn't really have a single thing to do with Christmas, did they? But as my Dad would say, "Whose care?"

Times change a lot, of course. Our family changed as aunts and uncles moved on to that big Christmas feast in the sky and cousins and friends moved away. We were dealt the biggest blow when Mom passed away in 2008. But the memories of those fond, fun, food-filled, family Christmases that she and Dad helped create will live forever. Even if we don't do the Seven Fishes anymore. Even if Dad doesn't wear the battery-powered bow-tie on Christmas Eve anymore. Even if we don't drink quite as much Strega anymore ...

Oh, wait. We still do drink quite a bit of Strega.

And we laugh. And we sing along to Lou Monte and Sinatra and even Elvis. We tell stories about Mom and Christmases past. We offer cheers. And we eat. Boy, do we eat. There usually is some kind of seafood present at our feast, which was held at my sister Teresa's for a few years and then at my sister Lisa's, not Mom and Dad's any longer. And there's also more meat than there ever used to be.

But that really is OK. Some things change. Some things stay the same.

Always, however, the door is open wide. Don't knock ... just come inside.

15

Hey, What Are You Made Of?

Dimmi con chi vai, e ti dirò chi sei. – *Old Italian proverb*

Said another way in Italian: *Per capire una persona guarda le persone che frequenta.*

Literally: Tell me who you hang out with and I will tell you who you are.

Duke Gorgoni had been a good friend of mine for a number of years. At one point, however – and quite unexpectedly, I must say – he became more than just a friend. He became a branch on my family tree.

His real name is Joseph Gorgoni, named after his father, but his nickname is Duke – and how is that for a great Italian handle, right? We met through a mutual friend, my lifelong buddy Kevin Hulslander, a lawyer in Syracuse, New York. Duke also is a lawyer, and that's how he knew Kevin.

We don't see each other as much as I'd like, but we manage to go to some Syracuse University basketball and football games together – including a handful of Big East tournaments in New York City – and we go out to dinner with our wives, getting together a handful of times a year. Thanks to the internet and texting, too, we are able to keep in touch fairly regularly.

Duke loves a lot of the same things that I do, especially all those fabulous things that come with our Italian heritage – he makes his own homemade wine, he loves cooking, making homemade macaroni and eating, especially in top-notch Italian restaurants. We always compare notes whenever we are together, whether it's on a new dish or a new batch of wine one of us made, whatever.

Around about 2005, Duke did some legal work for me, and as a means of partially repaying him, I set up a dinner at my Mom and Dad's house in Baldwinsville with Duke and his wife, Kevin and his wife, and my wife Jan and me. That may not sound like such a great form of remuneration to some, but the way my Dad could put out a spread, as you have been learning, it really was something special that I knew Duke would appreciate – everything from appetizers of bruschetta and pecorino cheese to homemade ravioli with braciola and meatballs to a roast with potatoes and vegetables, and of course, all the goodies in between.

The evening started, naturally, with introductions. My folks had never met Duke before.

"Mom and Dad," I said, "I would like you to meet a great friend of mine, Duke Gorgoni ..."

Dad shook his hand, Mom gave him and his wife a hug, and then she said, "What's that last name again?"

"Gorgoni," Duke replied.

"Are you any relation to Benny Gorgoni?" Mom asked, pulling out a name that I had never heard before in my life.

"He's my grandfather," Duke replied, somewhat stunned that she had come up with that name.

"Mick," Mom said, turning to me and using my nickname. "Duke is your cousin!"

Well, you probably can imagine the chorus of "WHATs?!?" and "HOLY COWs!?!" that echoed throughout the house with that declaration. I had known Duke for at least 10 years, always enjoyed being around him, loved comparing notes ... but ... cousins?

C'mon. Really?

It seems that Benny Gorgoni was married to one of Mom's aunts on her father's side. My maternal grandfather, Dominick Tucci, died when Mom was only six years old. She was the oldest of four children, but, at six, she remembered very little about him, unfortunately. And though he had seven brothers and four sisters, the Tucci name just did not come up an awful lot in our family discussions. Mom's mother re-married after her husband Dominick passed away, and Mom just sort of drifted away from the extended Tucci family, other than her brothers and sister, for the rest of her life. Anyway, one of grandpa's sisters – Mary Tucci – married Benedetto (Benny) Gorgoni, who was from the beautiful city of Lecce, in the Puglia region of Italy.

So Mary and Benny were my buddy – er, my cousin – Duke's grandparents.

That evening, with the fabulous dinner fashioned by Dad and the shocking story revealed by Mom, turned into one of the most memorable ones of my life. Isn't it funny how such things happen? It also made me begin to wonder more about family lineage, especially on Mom's side, which I was not nearly as familiar with as Dad's. Mom died in 2008 before DNA testing and profiling became a big thing and before my daughter and I had ours done, which has led us down so many fantastic and enlightening paths that we never knew existed.

I love those commercials for Ancestry.com in which the people say they thought their heritage was such-and-such, but then they have their DNA tested, and they find out they really are so-and-so. Don't you?

This is not meant to be a plug for Ancestry because I know there are other companies that will test your DNA – 23andMe, MyHeritage, LivingDNA come to mind – but I chose Ancestry perhaps because of those commercials. I got my daughter Kristine one of the kits for Christmas because she loves that sort of thing. We really thought the results were going to be kind of a slam dunk. After all, my two parents have only Italian roots — that we knew of, at least; Kristine's grandparents on her mother's side are a mixed bag, with her grandmother being Irish, Welsh and Italian and her grandfather German, Dutch, English and probably some other nationalities that we don't know.

The results were somewhat surprising — not really worthy of one of those great ads, but at least something that got us thinking and talking. And there's nothing wrong with that, right?

First off, Italian heritage was separated out only as Italy/Greece in Kristine's test results, mainly because the Greeks had such a heavy influence on Italy. So, her DNA turned out to be 33 percent Italy/Greece, which was the major portion of her makeup. Interestingly, a typical native of Italy/Greece is said to have 70-80 percent of that in their DNA, according to Ancestry.

Her second-largest portion was 30 percent "Europe West," which includes Belgium, France, Germany, the Netherlands and Switzerland. No real surprise there because of grandpop on her mom's side.

No, the biggest surprise was No. 3 — 17 percent of her DNA was labeled "West Asia," which basically is the Middle East and includes countries such as Iran, Iraq, Syria, Turkey, Saudi Arabia, Lebanon and Israel.

That really threw us for a loop until we read Ancestry's explanation: 56 percent of Italy/Greece natives have these West Asian countries in their DNA. 56 percent! To me, it illustrates the movement of civilization, beginning in the Middle East and spreading into the Mediterranean countries and then on north from there.

It all was incredibly interesting, I thought. But the coolest thing was the next largest breakdown: Six percent of my daughter's DNA is from Scandinavia. That includes, primarily, the countries of Sweden, Norway and Denmark. Now, we didn't know if that came from me or her mother's side, but my father — who was born and grew up in southern Italy — had blonde hair and blue eyes as a boy when everyone else around him had much darker hair and eyes. While my Dad was growing up, there was a big, strong Swedish soccer player starring in the Italian leagues, and people used to say that Dad resembled him when he played ball.

I always felt that there were some northern European influences in Dad — and by extension in me and my three sisters — whether Germanic or Nordic. No one else in the family believed that, nor are there any records going back far enough to be able to figure it out. But once Kristine's DNA came back the way it did, the logical next step was that her dad — as in me — had to get his analyzed, too, so that we could isolate what came from her mom and what came from me.

My results were not nearly as interesting as Kristine's, though they certainly confirmed a few things.

I am 90 percent Italian with Ancestry predicting a high probability that most of my Italian lineage comes from the Campania and Lazio regions, which is true. There was absolutely no northern European or Scandinavian influence, so that kind of tossed the thinking that Dad was descended from a Swedish soccer star out the window.

My next largest percentage was eight, and it was Caucasus, which includes Armenia, Azerbaijan, Georgia, Iran, Iraq, Syria and Turkey. The region is defined as that between the Black and Caspian seas and is traditionally the dividing line between Europe and Asia.

I thought that was fantastic and so have been on the lookout for my Azerbaijanian relatives named Raul, Elmin, Sabina or Elvira, which are among the most popular names in that country. I haven't found any yet, but I have a feeling they're out there.

The final two percent of my makeup is Greek, again, no surprise since Greece had such a monumental impact on Italy.

The most interesting part of my DNA report, though, was a listing of about 150 people who were in Ancestry's database – that is, they also had taken the DNA test – and who, based on their results and mine, Ancestry felt were relatives of mine. When I first saw that report on my computer, I figured I would take it with a grain of salt, but when I opened it, and saw the first person listed was none other than my daughter Kristine, I started rethinking things. Ancestry's confidence level was "extremely high" that this person listed was a child or parent of mine.

Well, they kind of nailed that, I thought.

The next two people on the list that Ancestry had a similarly "extremely high" level of confidence were related are two of my first cousins. One of them, I could not tell by the handle she was listed with, but when I wrote to her through the Ancestry website and explained who I was and the fact that our DNA results show we may be related, the first line of her reply was: Is this Mick?

Bingo.

It's not magic, that's for sure, but it is the magic of science that makes everything come together. And armed with all the info that Ancestry provided, I've been able to start up a family tree, which has reached to levels beyond anywhere I would have thought I could go when I started this project.

I had a difficult time finding my maternal grandfather, again because I knew so very little about him, but once I did and was able to plug him into the picture, the family tree self-pollinated with all his 11 brothers and sisters, and we were off and tree building. It is up to over 1,200 people at this point, and I really haven't even begun to dig into the folks on my Dad's side yet.

I have found my mother's maternal and paternal grandparents, so all four of my great-grandparents – names I never knew or heard growing up. And beyond that, tracing my paternal great-grandfather, I have found a great-great-grandfather and a great-great-great-grandfather. Ancestry has even gone so far as to give me a "potential" match for a great-great-great-great-grandfather, which I am looking into. He hails from Foggia, again in Italy's Puglia region, and was born in 1845. I'd say, with the success rate that I have had so far, I would be more surprised if that potential match was NOT a relative!

As for the Gorgoni clan – Duke, Benny and the rest – they occupy very prominent branches in my tree. Recently, on my sister Lisa's Facebook page, I noticed that she was "friends" with a Marisa Gorgoni. I wrote to my sister and told her that she and her friend Marisa may be more than friends, that they may be cousins.

She thought I was nuts because she – like me previously – had never heard that name in any family discussions. But then I told her about that dinner party at Mom and Dad's. And about Duke …

And yes, we have confirmed that Marisa also is a cousin of ours.

This family tree building process continues to be a work in progress, especially as Ancestry adds more people to its database. It's an interesting juxtaposition to me that one's family tree grows – or becomes more alive, if you will – by adding more and more dead people.

One of the folks listed as being a fourth or fifth or sixth cousin – with a very high degree of probability – is a woman named Tina Smith. I wrote to her, and she said that many of her relatives come from San Salvatore Telesino, and again, I thought, "Bingo." We haven't been able to connect all the dots exactly just yet, but at one point she told me that she had heard she was related to a Pope, and she thought it was Pope Pius XII who happened to be pope during World War II. She said that she thought one branch of her tree and one of mine might be related through Pope Pius.

I thought that was incredibly interesting and brought that information to my Dad. He thinks DNA is kind of a hocus pocus thing that he doesn't quite understand, but as he searched his memory banks, he said that he remembered his grandmother, Luigina Pacelli, saying that she – and then by extension him ... and me – was related to a pope. I said, "Well, pop, maybe we are, if what Tina is saying checks out and connects to your grandmother's people, there's our connection to the Vatican."

He kind of pooh-poohed it, which I understand. But just for the heck of it, I looked up Pope Pius' real name before he took a religious name when he became head of the Holy Catholic Church. His given name? Eugenio Maria Giuseppe Giovanni *Pacelli.*

You can't make this stuff up. Or actually, I suppose you could, but I'm not. So ever since I did that little bit of research, I have been going around blessing everyone. Why not?

Would you like more? Recently, while exploring my Dad's side, I came across a name of a guy who was one of his best friends growing up in San Salvatore Telesino, Anselmo Mattei. The birth and death dates were exactly the same as Anselmo's because the last time I visited his tomb in the San Salvatore Telesino cemetery I took a photograph of the plaque that adorned it. So, it is him! Right there on my tree. The branch that includes Anselmo – who was well-loved in the village, a long-time public servant who played a large role in setting up the festival in honor of the village's patron saint every year – followed from one of my Dad's uncles, a Luigi Cutillo.

I still haven't quite figured out if Anselmo is a direct relative or if he is related only through marriage, but I am excited about continuing to explore things.

As I do, I may be able to say to Dad someday, "Dad, you remember your buddy Anselmo? ... Well, he was your cousin!"

16

The Roots Run Deep
In Italia

La conoscenza ha radici amare ma dolci frutti. – *Italian proverb*
Literally: Knowledge has bitter roots but sweet fruits. *(Or... digging to find information might be difficult work, but it can have sweet rewards.)*

In the previous chapter, we looked at searching for – and discovering, at times – our Italian roots with some of the modern tools at our disposal, such as DNA analysis and the internet. In this chapter, we are going to look at the old-fashioned way – personal visits and face-to-face connections, *faccia a faccia* as they would say.

I am always amazed by how much folks in the Old Country go out of their way to help those who are looking for their relatives – and by how much they are thrilled when they can help make a connection. I don't know, maybe it's just another reason to have an extra glass of *vino* or a toast of *grappa* in celebration, but I think it's probably much more than that.

I'm not talking about my personal situation so much because I still have very close relatives in Italy, and when I visit, they take me around and introduce me to people, places and things that are connected to my past and my family. There's really no call for me to do much sleuthing.

I'm talking more about those who just take a shot – often sight unseen – at digging up some of the family soil.

On a flight from Rome to Naples once, I happened to be seated next to a man name Steve Briganti, who was about my age, mid-40s, and was heading to NSA Naples, a United States Naval base that is home to both the U.S. Sixth Fleet and the U.S. Naval Forces Europe. As we flew past Mount Vesuvius, he told me about a time, years earlier and fresh out of college, when he traveled to Italy to experience the land of his forefathers and to try to find relatives in a small village near the city of Potenza, which is in Basilicata, a mountainous region in the south that has some coastlines on both the Gulf of Taranto and the Tyrrhenian Sea; Potenza is the region's capital city.

Steve had barely stepped off the train in the little village and begun talking to local folks, asking about the Briganti name, when he was whisked to the town's central *piazza*. Not knowing much of the language at all, he mixed and matched with what little Italian he did know and some English and quickly made fast friends with the locals, bandying about various relatives' names and relating as much of the family story as his limited vocabulary would allow. Unfortunately, he learned there were no more Brigantis in town, though he was told that the family had enjoyed a long, successful run. Many family members were still remembered fondly.

Steve recounted how he was wined and dined by the townsfolk, who were so happy to have a young, successful American naval officer in their midst with ties to their village. They sang and danced, ate and drank all night and were especially proud to serve him a drink from their bar's top shelf – Kentucky bourbon.

So, even though he never got to meet anyone directly from his family, he was made to feel every bit as a part of that small village as any Briganti who had ever walked its streets.

A similar thing happened to me when I went to a small village about an hour from my Dad's in search of ancestors or relatives of a friend of mine from the United States. Some of John Gregoria's relatives had come from the small southern village of Santa Croce del Sannio, in the same Province of Benevento as Dad's San Salvatore Telesino; John's family's original surname was the un-Americanized "DiGregorio."

I was tooling around that day with my Uncle Louie Porto, my Mom's uncle whose family also was from San Salvatore Telesino. When we pulled into John Gregoria's village around midday *siesta* time, it was so quiet and serene, I'm quite sure you could have heard a *lira* drop on the cobblestone streets. We wandered around the main *piazza*, checking out the village's church and trying to stay quiet when two shutters opened from a second story window that was facing the square. An elderly man leaned out and asked us who we might be looking for. I told him the name, and he invited us up for an espresso and a glass of wine – not an unusual combination at all in Italy. We took him up on his graciousness, and it turned out the man was a retired attorney who knew a lot of the village's history. He knew of some DiGregorios, he told us, but said that we might have better luck if we went to the village deli to speak with its owner because he knew even more history or *storia*.

So, after our wine and coffee, we headed over to the deli, which was just reopening after the afternoon rest time. We told our story to the owner who immediately got on the phone – an old-fashioned one that was attached to the wall, by the way, kids – and within minutes had connected with someone in the DiGregorio lineage who, incredibly, invited us to join them for dinner that night. Sight unseen.

Our time was limited, though, and we had to decline, but I thought that in two very short hours or so, we had made some new friends, had enjoyed a lovely glass of wine, received a much appreciated dinner invitation, and had walked on the same dusty village streets where my friend John's relatives had once walked. All that, and neither I nor Uncle Louie were relatives!

Another Italian-American friend of mine from here in the States, Charlie Agonito, told me once that he and I must be *paisans* because his people had also come from a town in the Province of Benevento called Montesarchio.

On that same day trip with Uncle Louie, I noticed Montesarchio on the map – yes, folks, this was before Google and GPS, so it was a paper, folding map. The town was near the city of Benevento, and I figured it must be my friend's, so we cruised there too.

A pretty medieval town that had a Tuscan look to it, perched on a hilltop, Montesarchio, like San Salvatore Telesino, also dates back to the

Samnites and then the Romans. It has about 10,000 people and is perhaps most famous for a castle and tower just outside of town that offer spectacular views of the city and of the valley below.

Well known, too, for its main piazza with an ancient marble fountain, and that is where we stopped, discovering a quiet little café that was open right near the fountain. It was quiet there, too, that day, and we started up a conversation with a waiter. I told him about my friend, and he said he had heard of the name Agonito but did not know any.

Just then, in walked a few teenaged boys who started to play some video arcade games, and one of them – yes, believe it or not – was the splitting image of my friend Charlie! He was a bit thinner and quite a bit younger, but I did a double-take because he looked so much like him. With eyes wide open, I told the waiter that, and he went to speak to the young man on my behalf. The teen, whose name was Alessandro, told the man he didn't have any relatives that he knew of with the last name of Agonito, but he promised he would speak with his father that night and call me if they came up with a connection.

We exchanged phone numbers, and even though they never did call me back, it was a memorable experience that became even more memorable by something that happened while Uncle Louie and I were enjoying our cappuccinos.

A man pulled up in his Fiat right in front of the doorway to the café, which was on the left side of the street. He turned the motor off, and reclined back in his seat, while another one of the café's waiters walked over, shook his hand and had a conversation with him for a few minutes. The waiter left and returned after a few minutes with a bottle of Peroni beer – I knew it was Peroni, one of Italy's iconic brews, because of the green bottle. The man drank the beer and when he was finished, handed the empty bottle to the waiter. They spoke a bit more before the waiter left to fetch him another beer. When he returned, he handed it to the man, they clasped hands, said *arrivederci*, and the man drove off.

Uncle Louie and I didn't say much as we watched that little show, but we were both absorbing it. After the man left, we both laughed, and I asked him, "How many American laws did that man just break?" We did the accounting: pulling up on the wrong side of the street, a one-way street at that, then drinking an opening container of alcohol while parked, then driving away with another open container! Plus, we joked, neither of us noticed him putting on his signal light when he pulled away from the café, nor was he wearing a seatbelt.

This is not meant to reflect badly upon our beloved Italy, though some will take it as such. We just laughed, shook our heads and said, "This is a different kind of country."

When we asked our waiter who the man in the car had been, he said, "Oh, he's just the owner."

Anyway, back to digging for roots!

In 2005, during a group trip to Tuscany that I had organized, Dad and I and my great buddy Dan Chelenza and his wife Mary broke off for a few days to head to Vasto, a seaside town on the Adriatic coast in the region of Abruzzo. Dan's late father was born in Vasto, and even though no relatives remained – the aunts and uncles had all come to the United States when they were very young – he still wanted to see the town where his father was born and grew up. It was no short trip, about a six-hour drive from *Toscana,* but we broke it up by stopping about half-way at a town outside of Rome called Vicovaro to have lunch with our friend Sebastiano Lucci. Sebastiano, originally from Rome, is a professor at Hobart and William Smith Colleges in Geneva, New York, but was in Rome visiting relatives at the same time we were there. The funny thing was that even though Sebastiano had lived his entire life in Rome, he had never had occasion to step foot in Vicovaro, which was just 30 miles east of the Eternal City. We met and found a little trattoria that was just getting ready to close up for that *siesta* time, again. The owner said most menu items were no longer available, but he would have the cook – his wife – whip us up a meal of whatever she had remaining in the kitchen if we didn't mind. We didn't, and that was one of the best off-the-cuff lunches we'd ever had, right outside the pretty little town of Vicovaro, which is surely not on any tourist itinerary.

Speaking of adventures, though, we noted on another map – yet again, one of those large fold-out things that we spread on the table –

that there was a town called Celenza sul Trigno about 30 miles south-west of Vasto. Call me crazy, but I had a thought that maybe, just maybe, ALL Chelenzas originated from that small hill town on the Trigno River. Maybe, maybe not, but I thought we just had to go there. Danny agreed with a big smile.

So, after a beautiful night of wandering the main streets of Vasto and its sister seaside town of Vasto Marina, and dining on one of the most luscious, freshest seafood dinners we've ever had, the next day we motored on down to Celenza with Danny and Mary Chelenza.

(Quick language lesson here: "ce" in Italian sounds like "ch" as in "chair;" the "h" in Danny's "Chelenza" name probably was added to the

My buddy, Dan Chelenza (Americanized spelling), stands under a welcome sign to the mountaintop Abruzzo village of Celenza sul Trigno, which means Celenza on the Trigno River. It's my guess that the very surname of Chelenza or Celenza (Italian spelling) itself originated in this village in the Province of Chieti. At the very least, Dan, standing at 6-foot-6, is certainly one of the tallest people – whether Chelenza or Celenza – to stand beside that sign.

spelling in the United States so that it would be pronounced the same as the Italian version without the "h." So, *Celenza* in Italian is pronounced the same as *Chelenza* in English).

Our timing was similar to other adventures – that is, the four of us arrived in Celenza sul Trigno just about *siesta* time. We did, however, manage to find one little downtown bar that was still open. We explained to the owner about Dan's last name, and he was grabbing a phone book for us to look up others in town with the Celenza/Chelenza name when his phone rang. His wife said she had dropped the macaroni into the boiling water and was waiting on him for lunch. The owner seemed to enjoy chatting with us, but we all know when it's time to eat the macaroni, it's time to eat the macaroni. However, this is the incredible part of this story: He told us we could stay in his bar as long as we liked, thumb through the phonebook (even call some of the Celenzas who were listed in it if we so desired), and help ourselves to any other drinks or snacks that we wanted. He told us to leave any payment for the snacks on the counter and just close the door when we left because it would lock behind us – and away he zipped on his motor scooter to have his lunch, leaving us dumbfounded at his trusting and friendly nature.

You certainly could tell that it was *pranzo* – or lunch – time in the little village because as we sat with our drinks at an outdoor table, windows were open on the warm summer day, and we could easily hear the sounds of dishes being passed out, families talking and a Formula One race on numerous TVs (it being a Sunday and Formula One being almost as popular a sport in Italy as soccer).

We didn't stay very long at our new friend's bar, nor did we make any phone calls, but we walked the pretty little mountaintop village's cobblestone streets, looked at a War Memorial in a park that listed a few Celenzas as having died in the service of Italy, and took some photos of Dan next to signs that read "Celenza." How about that? Standing next to a sign with your last name on it?

Such is the never-ending magic of *bell'Italia*, whose roots – even for Italian-Americans – do indeed run deep.

17

A Friendship Struck Up
In A Whirlpool

Chi trova un amico, trova un tesoro. – *Italian proverb*
Literally: Whoever finds a friend, finds a treasure.

This tale could easily be entitled "You Never Know Where You'll Find Your Next Amico."

There I was, lounging in an outdoor whirlpool at a well-known spa in the pretty upstate New York village of Skaneateles (pronounced "skinny-ATLAS," an Iroquois word meaning "long lake"). I was minding my own business, sipping a glass of red wine – that's why I was in the whirlpool because it was located next to the bar, what else? – and waiting for my wife, Jan, who was having a pedicure.

While she was getting her toes lovingly attended to, my plan was to kick back in the whirlpool for a bit, then relax even more in the spa's cooler "quiet" area, and then possibly finish things up by hitting the dry sauna to sweat out those toxins.

That was the plan, at least, but I never even made it to stage two.

As I was sitting and sipping in the whirlpool, I heard something that one doesn't hear very often in upstate New York – downstate maybe, or in any number of big cities across America but not in the pretty little Finger Lakes village of Skaneateles: A conversation in Italian.

I would learn later the couple was speaking in Italian not because they didn't want anyone to know what they were talking about – it was just small talk about the unusually hot weather and the gorgeous spa itself – but because they felt more comfortable speaking in Italian. He was from Calabria, as it turns out, and she had studied in Florence. In fact, that beautiful, historic Tuscan city is where they had met a dozen or so years earlier.

So, me being me – that is, unable to let anything Italian pass by without investigating – I waded over to them in the pool, excused myself and asked if they were, as I suspected, Italian. He was a native, of course, and she had only studied there, but I complimented her on the way she spoke the language, which was impeccable. They invited me to sit with them for a while.

I did, and that is exactly how I spent the next hour as Jan's toes were fancied up.

The first 15 or 20 minutes of our conversation was in Italian, as I was just learning their story and didn't even know yet if they spoke English. It was great practice for me, again especially in a town like Skaneateles where I certainly did not expect to be working out my language skills that afternoon.

When the man finally broke into English, however, I was happy to go down that avenue, too. My Italian is pretty good, but I think my English is just a bit more, well, let's say expansive.

We had a lovely visit, and I learned that my new friend Pasquale was an architect. He and his wife Maria had been married for about 10 years, lived in Cortland (another upstate New York town) and also spent a lot of time in Schenectady, near Albany. I told them that Schenectady had a special – kind of silly – place in Jan and my hearts. She has some relatives who live there, Italian-Americans, of course, who have the reputation of being – how can I say this without proliferating old Italian-American stereotypes? – ruffians. Yes, ruffians, let's put it that way, but remember the reference is used in a joking sense, at least between us. When Jan finds herself in a difficult situation, especially with someone who is giving her a hard time or might not be giving her the assistance she is looking for, she'll say something like, "Hey, if you don't help me here, I know people in Schenectady who will pay you a visit." She says it threateningly but then breaks into a laugh, which is what Pasquale and Maria did when I finished my little tale.

Anyway, Schenectady aside, they told me they get back to Calabria often to visit his family. Meanwhile she was longing to return to Tuscany where they met.

I also learned that he was a huge soccer fan, a passion of mine, as well. In fact, as soon as I mentioned *calcio*, his eyes lit up, while she rolled hers. "Soccer?" she said. "Are you kidding me? That's all he thinks about."

It was 2008 and the European Soccer Championships were about to get underway that very weekend in Switzerland and Austria, so we had plenty to talk about as the warm water gurgled around us and the merlot slid down our throats. Pasquale told me that his hometown in Calabria is near Gennaro Gattuso's hometown. If you don't know Gennaro Gattuso, he was one of the stars of the Italian national soccer team at the time. Pasquale had even been to the sporting goods shop that Gennaro owned in Calabria. It was great fun talking to him about Gattuso, a feisty, aggressive, hard-driving player who was one of my favorites.

By that point, Jan's toes had been properly dolled up, and she was searching for me throughout the spa, looking in the spots where I had told her I might be. When she found me outside in the whirlpool – exactly where she had left me – she knew something must be up. I couldn't wait to introduce her to my new friends, which I did.

"I figured you must have met someone to still be in the whirlpool," she said with a laugh, and our new friends asked her about her cousins in Schenectady, which, of course, drew a quizzical look from her. Followed by some laughs after I explained that I had told them our "inside joke."

Pasquale and I exchanged email addresses and continue to stay in touch. We had lots of commiserating to do that year as Italy flopped out of those European Championships with a pitiful performance, but beyond soccer we have learned about each other's families and though we have never seen each other again, face to face, we hope to get together someday in Italy. Maybe in Calabria; maybe in Tuscany. Maybe even in San Salvatore Telesino.

And to think, it all started in the whirlpool.

18

Italian Culture in
The Big Easy? Yes!

Il mondo è un libro, e quelli che non viaggiano ne leggono solo una pagina.
– *Agostino d'Ippona*

Translation: Life is a book and those who don't travel read only one
page. – *Saint Augustine*

Whenever I'm on the road – and wherever that road may be
taking me, through the United States, to Italy, Germany, Switzerland,
wherever – I enjoy searching out all things Italian.

I even found a "Little Italy" section in San Diego long before it
was called that – and all the Italian restaurants were owned by Mexicans.
My Uncle Louie was living nearby in La Jolla at the time, and when he
came into San Diego to meet us he asked where we wanted to go for
dinner. When I said I wanted to check out "Little Italy," he said, "What
are you talking about? There is no Little Italy in San Diego." I showed
him a copy of that day's *San Diego Tribune* newspaper, which, in its fea-
ture section, had a large story about the city's developing "Little Italy."
Uncle Louie said, "How about that? I've lived here for 10 years and never
knew there was such a thing. You're here for 10 minutes and you find
this … *mannaggia.*"

Well, it's what I do.

Uncle Louie had wanted to take us to some famous seafood restaurant, but instead – not ever one to turn down Italian – he happily went
along with our request. We ended up finding a great little joint, one of
which that had been profiled in the paper that had everything from red-

and-white checkered tablecloths to carafes of red table wine. The meal was exceptional, and we learned that it was, indeed, owned by Mexicans. That didn't matter to me as I had one of the best plates of *spaghetti alle vongole* – spaghetti with clams – that I've ever had.

I've had similar experiences in the Italian sections of cities such as Pittsburgh, Seattle, Buffalo, Boston and of course New York City – and in the Big Apple, you can choose which borough you'd like to explore for Italian culture, the Bronx (Arthur Avenue area is the best), Manhattan (everyone knows Mulberry Street), Brooklyn (I love Bensonhurst), Queens (Corona is the neighborhood), Staten Island (well, I think pretty much all of Staten Island!).

My sister Teresa lives in Florida these days, and whenever we visit her on the Gulf Coast, she always takes us to her favorite Italian delicatessen. My daughter Kristine lives in North Carolina, where it's not particularly easy to find great Italian spots. But she has managed to, though.

The point is that there are so many places in these great United States that have connections to Italy, even many that you don't think would have such a connection.

In the early spring of 2018, my wife and I were getting ready for a trip to New Orleans – our first visit to the Big Easy – and we asked our friends, Paul and Lisa Barrett, the folks we were traveling with, if there was an Italian section or neighborhood there. Paul had lived and worked in or near the city for a good dozen or so years and said that he didn't really know of any.

Of course, harkening back to Uncle Louie, I said, "Yeah, I've heard that before."

Really, all his answer did was just make me more determined to see what I could find out, and what I learned was incredibly interesting.

New Orleans may not have a Little Italy, per se, at least not now. But over 100 years ago, it had a bustling, vibrant Italian section. You may have heard of it. These days it's called the French Quarter!

That's right. While most people think of New Orleans as having been built by the French and Spanish, it was actually the Italians – and specifically, the Sicilians – who helped build the city into what it is today. The oldest groups of Italians settled into New Orleans before the Civil War, and many of those *paisans* even ventured up into the Mississippi Delta to work the incredibly fertile land there.

Then, in the 1870s and '80s, a larger wave of Italian immigrants – in fact, 290,000 from 1884 to 1924 – flowed into the Crescent City, bringing with them their culture, their work ethic, their social clubs and benevolent organizations, and yes, even, unfortunately, organized crime. The most infamous and powerful of the mafioso may have been Carlos Marcello – born Calogero Minacori to Sicilian parents – who ruled the city's crime family from 1947 until the late 1980s.

The abundant Sicilian connection came from the fact that there was a direct transatlantic boating line from Palermo to New Orleans. So many Sicilians went to New Orleans and settled in what is now the French Quarter that it was known as "Little Palermo" at one point. In the late 1800s there were more Italian immigrants in New Orleans than any city in America, including New York, Philadelphia and Boston.

It excited me to learn all that, and I couldn't wait to tell my New Orleans friends. They were astonished.

There is no Little Palermo there these days because many of the Italians moved into other neighborhoods or the suburbs, rather than be concentrated in one area, but their influence on the city was unmistakable.

The Sicilian tradition of elaborate St. Joseph's Day tables is now a New Orleans tradition as well; so much so that many who celebrate and revel in it, don't even realize it's Italian, they think it's something that just started in New Orleans. Progresso Foods, an offshoot of a French Quarter grocery store run by a Sicilian immigrant, started there. Of course, many of you know that the late jazz great Louis Prima was from there.

The elegant Hotel Monteleone, one of the city's oldest and most famous with its revolving Carousel Bar, was founded by a Sicilian shoemaker. It's a must-see in the French Quarter and is still run by the Monteleone family.

And one of New Orleans' iconic food items – the muffuletta sandwich – naturally was an Italian concoction. I say naturally because the name alone gives away its origin. In 1906, Salvatore Lupo, who ran Central Grocery on Decatur Street, combined meats such as mortadella and ham with cheese and an olive salad on loaves of fresh, round Italian bread. They were ideal for laborers – especially Sicilian workers – on the go. And today, few go to New Orleans without sampling a muffuletta; or two. Lines start forming at Central Grocery first thing in the morning, before the store even opens!

Also, in 1978, renowned architect Charles Moore designed the Piazza D'Italia on the corner of Tchopitoulas and Poydras streets, a piazza and a monument – with a Roman-column style promenade – to celebrate the contributions of the Italians to New Orleans. A scene in the 1986 movie "The Big Easy" with Dennis Quaid, Ellen Barkin and John Goodman was filmed there. However, many folks – including those who have lived their whole lives in New Orleans – don't even know it's there; my friends didn't.

But my wife Jan, my sister Teresa, our friend Angelea and I took a walk to it one afternoon to pay homage and say, *"Ah salute."*

Interestingly, too, the very street where we stayed on that trip – Orleans Street – also had some history, though not particularly good history. In 1890 New Orleans Police Chief David Hennessy was gunned down, allegedly by two Italians. It resulted in a manhunt that led to the arrest of 250 Italian immigrants with 19 eventually named in connection to the murder. They were locked up in a prison that is where the Municipal Auditorium is now located in the Quarter, and one account I read online said a "mob made its way down Orleans Street in the French Quarter, passed Congo Square, and arrived at the prison. They hounded to be let in."

That led to one of the largest lynchings in the city's history, and while that is a dark and sad story, it still shows how much of an impact the Italians had on the Big Easy.

They are still making an impact, in fact, because as this book was being written – on April 12, 2019 – New Orleans Mayor LaToya

Cantrell formally apologized for the lynching, although it was long before she even was born. She said what happened to those Italians was "wrong, and the city owes them and their descendants a formal apology."

She made the apology at the American Italian Cultural Center in the Central Business District at a podium with an Italian flag next to it, saying, "At this late date, we cannot give justice, but we can be intentional and deliberate about what we do going forward."

Some said the apology was too little and way too late, but many others praised Cantrell, who was the first New Orleans mayor to recognize and address the long-ago injustice.

So, there you have it, even the city of jazz, the city of Louie Armstrong, the city of the Saints, and Bourbon Street and the French Quarter, has a strong connection to Italy. So, the next time you are in New Orleans, make sure you check into that Italian influence … maybe while nibbling on a muffuletta and listening to Louie Prima.

ALTRE STORIE DI PAPÀ

OTHER STORIES ABOUT DAD

19

Dad, World War II and Montecassino

Di guerra, caccia e amuri, pri un gustu milli duluri. – *Sicilian proverb*

Literally: In war, hunting, and love you suffer a thousand pains for one pleasure.

There are books and websites filled with quotations on war from Fascist Italian dictator Benito Mussolini, but – even though he was a journalist at one point, just like me – I don't want to give the impression that I favor him or his ideology in any way. That is why I stayed away from all those sayings and instead selected the old Sicilian proverb that tops off this chapter.

To me, one of the only good things that comes from war is banding together to fight for a common cause, even if accomplishing that goal causes an incredible amount of suffering, as the proverb suggests.

I recognize that war often is necessary, but it is rarely a good thing.

However, to a young boy, unfazed by the horrors of the fighting because of that very youth, it can be intriguing, interesting and maybe even somewhat entertaining.

So it was for my father, who turned from a young boy into a teenager during the World War II years; his 13th birthday was in May of 1944, just five months before Italy surrendered to the Allies and declared war on Nazi Germany, its one-time Axis partner. While boys his age in the United States only heard about the fighting and the battles in Europe from adults or from static-filled radio reports, Dad lived through it all and remembers everything very well.

We are reminded of that often while watching news coverage of conflicts around the world today. The images often lead me to wonder how, decades from now, the kids who survive in war-torn places such as Afghanistan and Baghdad and Syria will remember what they have witnessed first-hand, as well, and what they will tell their children and grandchildren.

Perhaps most interesting are Dad's recollections of Mussolini, who ruled Italy with an iron hand. After partnering with Adolf Hitler, Mussolini dragged his country into a war that many Italians did not want.

Dad has come to learn about many of the atrocities committed by Mussolini and his regime, primarily through history books, movies and documentaries. However, as a young boy, all he knew was that on Saturday mornings, he and his young pals got to march in a parade through the village, dressed in shiny new uniforms provided, directly, by "*Il Duce.*"

Of course, it was part of Mussolini's way to indoctrinate the youngsters and to get them to look favorably upon him and his propaganda. The young boys didn't know – or care – about all that. All they knew was they felt like heroes as they marched through the dusty streets of the poor village of San Salvatore Telesino in those crisp uniforms – different colors for different age groups – cheered on by their mothers and fathers, aunts and uncles.

After the parade, they would be treated to ice cream and other treats.

Later, at home, they would hear the adults rave about how Mussolini was making life in Italy so much better, how hospitals were being built, schools were going up, roads were being improved, and in the south, the terrifying mafia was even being subdued, many said because Mussolini's armed Blackshirts were even more ruthless than members of the crime syndicate.

Ruthless dictator? Not to a lot of folks, some who even saw him as a benevolent humanitarian. When the war itself rolled into Italy, in general, and into places like Dad's tiny southern farming village, in particular, Michele and his young friends and cousins were hardly frightened.

At times, they would lounge in the fields, munching on chestnuts or popping grapes into their mouths, while hundreds of B-17 or B-24 bombers lumbered above them, sometimes completely blocking out the otherwise bright-blue skies. The kids wondered not so much about the destruction that those bombers could spawn but rather who was the best soccer player in the world, or they would debate about whose *mamma* or *zia* made the best gnocchi.

Many times at night, they would watch bombs going off in the distant mountains and gaze upon them as some sort of fireworks show. It was as if they were shielded from the reality much in the way actor Roberto Benigni safeguarded his young son from the horrors of concentration camp life in the Academy Award-winning film "Life Is Beautiful."

Some other of Dad's most vivid memories include when Italy finally escaped the clutches of Nazi Germany, when the Italian people cast Mussolini aside and the country decided to join forces with the Allies in October of 1944. The Nazis had interwoven their way into almost every village, town and city in Italy – one day, they had been friends and compatriots of the Italians, fighting side by side for the Axis powers, and the very next day, or so it seemed to many, they were enemies. Just like that, just like someone flipped a switch.

While Allied troops fought to liberate Italy on major battlegrounds, in small villages such as Dad's, the townsfolk suddenly were frightened by the threatening Nazis. My grandfather and other men of the village had to head to the mountains, to hide from the new enemy. Sometimes, in those early days of their changed world, they remained there and away from their families for weeks at a time.

San Salvatore Telesino meant absolutely nothing in the overall scheme of the war, but the Nazis still thought they had to show their authority and their might, and Dad used to tell me about how they would blow up bridges, even in small villages. He told me, for years, about one bridge that crossed a stream on his family's farmland and became victim to the Nazis' power and might.

Dad never served during a war, but here he is shown in uniform as he satisfied his required military duty as a young man. He was a radio operator on the island of Sardinia.

A few years ago, I finally saw that bridge in person, and I couldn't believe my eyes. What the Nazis had destroyed was a foot bridge, really, that only affected about three farm families and their donkeys. The stream over which it crossed was about four feet wide and could be jumped over quite easily. I know, because I did.

Atrocities of war? More like absurdities of war.

Sure, if a tank were to roll through that terrain, it would be more difficult without the bridge, but as it was, the only problem it caused was for the poor farmers who needed to get their zucchini and their onions and tomatoes to market.

All things considered, though, the day that Italy was liberated completely from the Nazis was one of the best days of my Dad's – and therefore, of my family's – life.

Francesco Nicotra wrote about it in an op-ed piece in an edition of *Italy Italy* magazine: "I was only seven years old, but I clearly remember that day in 1944 when the American troops entered Rome, which was finally liberated from the nightmare of war and the Nazis. The GIs marched through the city, smiling broadly. On either side stood the crowd, shouting, clapping, crying, laughing and hugging one another. Sometimes, one of the soldiers would respond to the applause with a few words of an imperfect Italian."

Now that is a parade I would love to have witnessed.

One of World War II's most horrific battle sites was only 45 miles north of Dad's village, and in fact, when he talks of laying in the fields and watching scores of bombers fly overhead, I wonder if they might have been going to that site, which was Montecassino.

We know, of course, that Italy is filled with great things – food comes to mind, so do wine, incredible views, warm people. But what our favorite Old Country may have more of than anything else is history. Italy is home to more UNESCO World Heritage sites – 47 of them in 2018 – than any other country in the world. From historic city centers in Florence, Siena and San Gimignano to Roman ruins, the Tivoli Gardens and Greek temples in Agrigento, Sicily, some of that history dates back over 2,000 years.

Other sites – such as World War II landmarks in Anzio, Salerno and Sicily – aren't UNESCO sites and are only a handful of decades old but are every bit as historic and fascinating.

One site that combines those two histories – ancient and recent – is the Abbey at Montecassino, about 80 miles south of Rome.

Anytime I drive south from the Eternal City to San Salvatore Telesino on the A1 Autostrada, nicknamed the Highway of the Sun, I drive past the abbey high above the Liri Valley, usually glistening bright white in that Italian sun.

A few times over the years, I have ventured off the highway, into the city at the foot of the mountain, Cassino, and then made my way up the winding road to Montecassino. The first time I ever visited the abbey was with Dad and my Uncle Louie. Most recently in 2016, I went with my daughter Kristine. It never fails to captivate me. High above Cassino, a noisy, bustling town of about 37,000 people, Montecassino originally was noted as the site where St. Benedict built his first monastery, the source of the Benedictine Order, in 529 A.D.

It was sacked and burned down – at least parts of it – many times over the centuries, including in 1799 by Napoleon's troops. Then in 1944, it was the site of that famous and important – not to mention deadly and controversial – battle. As the Allied troops, led by the United States, marched toward Rome, the Germans had an impenetrable line of defense that stretched basically from one side of Italy to the other, from the western Mediterranean Sea to the eastern Adriatic Sea; Montecassino was an important part of that Gustav Line.

From high above, it was a perfect defensive perch for the Nazis. The Allies realized its impassable nature as well, and with the Nazi troops dug in there, it was decided they needed to be forcefully removed if the Allies were going to have any chance to continue on into Rome and liberate it. It took four attacks, one each in January, February, March and May of 1944, and cost 190,000 lives – including thousands of civilians in the city below and in the monastery – but eventually Montecassino was taken, the Nazi's Gustav Line was broken, and the Allies' advance continued. About a year later, the war was over.

The historic and beloved monastery, however, was destroyed by the bombings. Ironically, and this is where the controversy lies, it was determined later that the Nazis had not been in the building as was thought but rather had been holing up in various caves around the mountain. In February 1944, when 229 American bombers attacked, only monks and refugees, mostly women and children, were in the vaults of the abbey, which was demolished by 500 tons of explosives. After the February bombing left the monastery in shambles, the Germans did move into it, but it was easier for the Allied troops to fight them with the building basically obliterated, and again, the deadliest war in world history lasted only a few more months.

Then something amazing and incredible happened … little by little the abbey, remarkably, was rebuilt. It was reconsecrated by Pope Paul VI in 1964. Eighteen years after the horrific battle, a man named Harold L. Bond, who fought at Montecassino as an officer with America's 36th Infantry, Texas Division, returned to the site with his wife and four daughters. His visit resulted in a gripping book, "Return to Cassino: A combat veteran revisits the scenes of bloody battles and recalls the horrors and heroism of war."

While so many veterans refuse to talk about those horrors upon their return home, even to their families and close friends, Bond does, as he writes, "to show what war was like in Italy in 1944."

"Monte Cassino has haunted my mind for the past twenty years … this was the worst combat of the entire war for me, and during the long years of peace that followed, memories of it came back again. Scenes and incidents which I would have been happy to forget remained disconcertingly vivid."

Bond writes colorfully and factually, so much so that the reader can sense what an awful, frightening place Montecassino was during those times.

Today, however, it is again a beautiful, serene and wondrous monument to peace and serenity, belying that violent past. The monks who inhabit it are guided by two principles: prayer and work.

My daughter and I talked about that, to be sure in quiet, respectful tones, as she bent down and fed the dozens of pearly white doves that waddled over to her outstretched hand.

"From all the destruction," Kristine observed, "a beautiful, peaceful place like this arose."

She couldn't have been more right.

Yes, Italy has an incredible amount of history, dating back to antiquity, some of it violent, some of it creative and wondrous. All of it worth exploring.

20

Singing with the Choir ... Sort of

Un vocabolario può contenere solo una piccola parte del patrimonio di una lingua. – *Giacomo Leopardi, Italian philosopher, poet and essayist*

Literally: A dictionary can embrace only a small part of the vast tapestry of a language.

By now, wandering through these pages, you have met our somewhat bilingual Dad. You know that he has called a convertible a "portable." He has referred to the historic first president of the United States as a home appliance, namely "George Washing Machine." His all-time favorite musical instrument is the "cor-DEEN," which would be the *accordion* to you and me. He is notorious for chopping off the endings of words so that "corner" becomes "corn" – as in "Hey, Joey, meet me over there on the corn." And "pocket" turns into "pock" – "Here's a couple a bucks, put 'em ina your pock." One of our favorites is "ridiculous," which, when he says it, rhymes with "pickle," as in, "I can't believe the price of dat milk; it's a ridickle." Seriously. Sometimes when we're sitting around drinking wine with peaches, we'll try to think of off-the-wall, crazy scenarios to relate to Dad just so he'll say, "No way, dat's a ridickle."

We've had some good-natured fun in the family over the years ribbing Dad about the way he speaks English, but please, don't get me wrong, we wouldn't do it if he didn't take it as well as he does. He laughs at himself probably more than we do. Plus, he knows how incredibly proud we all are of him – how he came to America knowing only those handful of words in English, and now, six decades later, he can tell a tale

Dad plays a tune on the "cor-DEEN," which would be an accordion to everyone else.

as well as any native speaker. If not better. So what if he chops up some words or uses a phrase that's a little ridickle?

I remember one time in 1990 when we were visiting the Old Country and sitting around for dinner with a bunch of friends and relatives, and my Zio Enzo, Dad's only and older brother, a career military man, was asking me questions as to what I thought about my father. I was trying to think of a way to relate how intelligent I thought Dad was, even though he had made his living in America by working a simple blue-collar job in a machine shop. Then it struck me. I asked my Zio, "How many languages can you speak?"

"Well, I know a few words of English, a few words of French, maybe a little Spanish, but I can only speak Italian," Zio replied.

I proudly said, "Well, Dad speaks two languages fluently, Italian and English, and that second one he taught himself. He can tell a story equally as well in English as he can in Italian. And this from a guy who only went to school through the fourth grade. That's how intelligent I think my Dad is."

My Zio, a well-educated, intelligent man himself, thought about that for a moment and declared with his usual gusto and fist-pound on the table, "You are right, you are right! Speaking a second language fluently is not easy to do. Your father is *really* smart!"

So, we established that with the folks sitting around the table that evening, but to this day, a good 60 years since he first set foot on American soil, the bottom line is that Dad still manages to mangle the English language every now and again, and it just may be even funnier now than ever.

This episode happened relatively recently. My sister Teresa tells it best, but in her absence and since this is my book, please allow me:

Teresa had popped in on Dad for a quick visit, and he announced, in his heavy, thick accent, "Eh, I saw your a frienda Sherry [writer's note: name changed to protect the innocent] at the choir prack today."

"Choir practice?" Teresa replied. "Wow, I've known Sherry for a long time, and I didn't think she could even carry a tune, much less join a choir. I really wouldn't expect that you'd bump into her at choir practice. Are you sure that it was Sherry you saw, Pop, and not some-one else?"

"Yes. I say hello to her, and she say hello right back at me," Dad replied.

"And are you sure it was at choir practice?" Teresa asked.

Growing just a tad indignant, Dad replied: "Hey, come on, now. I might no talk all dat good, but I know where I go today. It was the choir prack. And that's where I saw your frienda Sherry."

Teresa kicks herself to this day because she did not ask Dad what I thought would have been this pertinent and logical follow-up question: What in the world were *YOU* doing at choir practice, Dad? That might have cleared things up rather quickly because Dad has never had any inclination of joining any sort of choir ... unless it was full of *cor-DEENs,* of course.

But she didn't ask. Instead she was just thinking how ridickle the whole thing was and that the next time she saw her friend Sherry she had to ask her when she had joined the choir, of all crazy things.

Within a few short days Teresa did get together with her friend, and the conversation went something like this:

Teresa: "Hey, Sherry, how long have you been singing in the choir?"

Sherry: "The choir? What are you talking about?"

Teresa: "Yeah, come on, the choir. The last time I saw my Dad he said that he saw you recently at choir practice."

Sherry: "Your Dad? Geez, I haven't seen your Dad in months."

Teresa: "Wow. Are you sure? That's strange because he swore it was you. He said you even said hello to him."

Sherry: "Oh, wait ... yes, yes ... I *DID* see your dad ... it was three or four weeks ago. That's right, I forgot. I bumped into him at the chiropractor's office!"

Teresa: "The chiropractor?"

Sherry: "Yes, yes, the chiropractor. I was leaving after my appointment, and I think your Dad was just coming in for his ... Now, what was that about me singing in the choir?"

Teresa: "Never mind."

21

Pack Your Bags … Or At Least Keep An Eye On Them

Le nostre valigie ammaccate erano di nuovo ammucchiate sul marciapiede; avevamo più modi per andare. Ma non importa, la strada è vita.

– American novelist Jack Kerouac

Literally: Our battered suitcases were piled on the sidewalk again; we had longer ways to go. But no matter, the road is life.

Dad made over fifty trips back to the Old Country, as has been noted in other chapters in this collection. The first one didn't come until 1968 – after he had been in the United States for 10 years. He took mom's Uncle Rudy to Italy, primarily to see family. By all accounts, it was a fabulous trip, full of laughs, tears and glasses of wine. And yes, *that* was the Uncle Rudy Gonnella who had been slated to go on that fateful trip to Italy in 1955 that Mom ended up going on instead and wound up meeting her future husband.

Something occurred as Uncle Rudy and Dad returned to the States after that '68 trip, however, that would become Dad's calling card for most of the rest of his traveling life: a luggage screw-up.

On that trip, as he packed to come home to America, he had loaded up his suitcases with all kinds of Italian foodstuffs – cheeses, a couple bottles of his father's homemade wine, his cousin's extra-virgin olive oil, bread baked from a brick oven, probably even some cured meat (though that was illegal to bring back into the States … shhhhh!) He had called Mom and told her to round up some friends and relatives and let them know that when he arrived back home, they would all dig in together.

I was a youngster and don't remember the scene, but I can picture it by the way Dad tells it. When he walked through the front door – a conquering hero like Caesar making his way under the victory arch – the family cheered. After greeting him, they all made their way around the dining room table, tucked napkins into collars, sharpened the eating utensils in their hands by rubbing them together, and waited with eyes wide open as Dad plopped his suitcase in the center of that table. Showman that he was, Dad embellished the moment by pointing to the suitcase and saying, "Oh boy, you won't believe what's in here ..."

"Open it, open it," the diners cried.

"Oh, it's some of the best stuff Italy has ... this is stuff you can't get over here ..."

"Open it, open it," the relatives could barely contain themselves.

Dad unlatched the suitcase and opened it slowly, again for dramatic effect. Then, as the story goes, he hoisted out ... a frilly piece of ladies lingerie, holding it up by the thin shoulder straps.

The relatives started with cat calls, and I can only imagine the quizzical look on my mother's face about what that slinky thing was doing in there, her head tipped to one side, an eyebrow raised.

"OK," Dad said, clearing his throat. "I don't know where that came from, but let's move on."

Then he pulled out ... a lovely woman's dress and then ... a silk blouse.

More catcalls from the gathered – and drooling – family. More wondering looks from Mom.

Dad forged ahead, now with more steam and determination. Where's that cheese? Where's that olive oil? Yet, all that came out were more women's clothes, a beautiful new leather purse, some silky undergarments, more lingerie, and stylish stilettos, doubtless purchased in Milan or Florence, those centers of Italian haute couture.

"C'mon, Mike, stop kidding around," the folks screamed, almost in unison.

Later in life, Dad loved using the phrase made famous in a Wendy's hamburger commercial: Where's the beef? That phrase wasn't part of the American lexicon quite yet in 1968, but if it were, I could have imagined my aunts and uncles saying it to Dad, in a teasing sort of way.

"C'mon, Mike, where's the beef?"

Or where's the capicola?

Well, after a few more minutes of this – with Dad as bamboozled as anyone – it became apparent that there would be no "Taste of Italy" at the dining room table that day.

Dad called the airport and was told that a young woman – with a suitcase of the exact same make, size and color as his – had grabbed it and must have taken it home by mistake.

I like to imagine that she had a house full of girlfriends over upon her return and was excited to show them the latest items of Italian fashion that she had brought home from her trip – just as Dad was hoping to show off the food products. And one by one, instead of those shiny new shoes, she pulled out a hunk of pecorino cheese … and then a bottle of green extra-virgin olive oil … and next a lovely salami.

I don't know if that's the case, of course, but one can certainly hope.

Dad went back to the airport the next day with her case and exchanged it for his own, which she also had returned. The relatives, however, did not reconvene for another grand unveiling. Being burned once was enough, and the luster was tarnished.

Dad's luck with luggage did not get much better over the years.

We started one trip with a flight from Syracuse to New York City, but our small, propeller-powered plane was detoured to Albany because of bad weather and because it was too heavy. The pilot told us that a few bags of luggage were going to have to be removed, though he assured us they all would end up at everyone's final destinations. As the baggage handlers were hauling out some of the suitcases in the darkness and the pouring rain, Dad looked over my shoulder and out the window from high above in the plane, and exclaimed, "Hey, they're taking off one of my suitcases."

"Calm down, Dad," I said. "I don't think that's yours. I mean, what are the chances?"

"Yes, it is," he said. "It is, I can see."

"No, it's not, but don't worry; if it is, it will end up in Naples with the rest of our bags," I said. "There's really not anything we can do about it now."

I didn't think of that bag the rest of the trip, which included an overseas flight from John F. Kennedy airport in New York to Leonardo DaVinci Airport in Rome, and then a smaller flight from Rome to Naples. I'm quite sure, though, that Dad was thinking about it all the way.

When we arrived in Naples – well, you can probably guess the ending of this story – three of our four bags were there waiting for us on the luggage carousel. The one that wasn't was the one Dad had spotted being taken off way back in rainy Albany.

We filed the first of many missing luggage reports and were assured that when it showed up, it would be delivered to San Salvatore Telesino, where we were staying.

It eventually did make it to the village but not for three or four days, as I recall, and in that one particular piece of luggage were all of Dad's extra pairs of pants. So, until it arrived, he wore the same pair and told the same story ... over and over.

We flew to Switzerland one time to visit Edmondo Pacelli, the best man in Dad's wedding who had moved there from San Salvatore Telesino, and this time, neither of Dad's two bags arrived along with us. Both of mine were there; Dad's not so much. Are you starting to see a pattern here? We filed a lost luggage claim in the Zurich airport and again were assured that we would receive a phone call when the bags showed up and that they would then be delivered to Edmondo's small Swiss village of Wittinsburg.

Dad had me phone the airport every day for three days. The luggage was never there, but they kept telling me, "Don't worry, when it shows up, we'll call you. And we'll deliver it."

On the fourth day, I called again. The person I was speaking with in the luggage claim office said she still hadn't seen anything that resembled Dad's bags, but while I was talking to her, I saw out the window, a delivery vehicle pull into Edmondo's driveway. Dad's missing suitcases were dropped off. There had been no phone call, but at least they made it. I sarcastically thanked the young woman on the phone for making it all happen, but she obviously had no idea what I was talking about.

Later, in the years long before "racial profiling" became a thing, I swear that Dad was pegged by American customs officials as a "person of interest" – that is, an older Italian man returning from the homeland; they probably could wager he had a salami or two in his suitcase.

So, on almost every trip, Dad invariably would be called over by those inspectors for a thorough hand-search of his luggage, and by association, because I was traveling with him, they would search through mine, too. Usually, their suspicions proved correct, and Dad, indeed, had stuffed a salami or some mortadella or a hard sausage or some other cured meat in a sock or a pant leg or a shirt sleeve.

Those officials would always find them, and I would always tell him, "Pop, you *know* you can't bring that stuff back with you."

He would look at me sheepishly and shrug his shoulders. It was sort of a, "Hey, you never know" look. Along with, "That's a dumb law anyway."

I think the only time I ever saw a tear in his eye – before Mom died, that is – was when he thought he had cleverly gotten away with sneaking a couple of good-sized salamis past the customs inspectors at JFK. Not so fast. We thought we were scot-free and on our way to a connecting flight, when a meat-sniffing beagle caught a whiff of Dad's suitcase, plodded over to us and put his nose right up against that case.

The beagle's handler, another customs agent, made like Howie Mandel on "Deal or No Deal" when he asked Dad to, "Please, open the case." When he did, the inspector discovered not one but both of those salamis in there. This was clearly "No deal" as far as the agent was concerned. He shook his head, cast a "sir, you just can't do that" look at Dad and told him he would have to take those two luscious homemade salamis away from him.

I must admit, they were real beauts, and Dad just couldn't rationalize them being confiscated. He went into "Deal" mode.

"What are you going to do with them?" Dad asked the inspector.

"Sir, these will be discarded," the man replied curtly but politely.

"Hey, listen," Dad said in hushed tones, looking over his shoulder as if he were making a drug deal. "How about you take one, and you let me take the other one? No one has to know ..."

"Sir, I can't do that," the inspector said. "That's a bribe."

"Listen, I'll bet you have a nice family, no?" Dad's negotiations continued. "Why don't you take one of these home for your wife and kids for dinner tonight? They were made with the most beautiful meat ..."

"Sir!" the agent interrupted. "That is not legal, and I could fine you for trying to smuggle them in. If you insist on continuing, there are going to be some consequences."

So, with me tugging at his shirt and saying, "C'mon, Dad, give it up," he turned over the two prized salamis. Of course, he had to get in the last words as we walked away: "I know he's not gonna throw those away ... he's a gonna take them home for his family tonight ..."

"Let it go, Dad, let it go."

He lost out on the deal, but I think Howie Mandel would have been proud.

That is how so many of our trips went over the years until Dad got older and came up with what he thought was the greatest scheme known to mankind, or at least to meat-smuggling, traveler-kind: I'm talking about, of course, wheelchair assistance in the airport.

After a neck operation, back and knee issues and the advancement in age, the last six or seven trips over, Dad always requested assistance in getting through airports. He seriously needed the help physically, but a side benefit, he realized after the first such experience, was that the wheelchair handlers were able to almost literally whisk him through different lines and different gates usually without the extensive scrutiny of luggage to which able-bodied walkers were subjected.

It may have had something to do with the fact that he looked old and feeble, so that the inspectors and agents would look more sympathetically upon him. Don't think he didn't play that card.

He also would have a friend, a butcher in San Salvatore Telesino named Salvatore, slice up those salamis and capicolas very thinly and then vacuum-seal them in slim, flat packages, which Dad slipped under his clothes in his suitcases as he packed.

So, here was the new meat-smuggling formula: No more big hunks of meat + Compassionate agents = Clear sailing through customs.

It's worked perfectly, I must admit. Too bad all the friends and relatives from that first 1968 scene aren't around any longer because in recent years, every return trip from Italy includes pulling out all kinds of nicely packaged meats from his suitcase. He usually hasn't even unpacked his clothes when he is taking out a thin package of vacuum-sealed prosciutto, opening it, grabbing a loaf of bread and making himself a snack. It's like he has a delicatessen packed in his bags. Even if he's not hungry, it's as if he has to – needs to – taste that luscious meat to prove that it did, indeed, accompany him to America.

One more bag story didn't have anything to do with cured meats. It had to do with candy.

Dad always likes to bring American-made gifts to his relatives and friends in Italy, and he makes a big production out of handing them out when we are sitting around a dinner table, like he is *Babbo Natale* or Santa Claus. In particular, he loves dishing out good old American-made chocolates.

On a 2012 trip, he had forgotten to load up on candy while he was packing his regular suitcase, so he stuffed oodles of it into his carry-on bag. And when I say stuffed, I mean so much was crammed in, there wasn't room for even another scrap of paper in that bag, much less a caramel or Peppermint Pattie.

As usual, we departed first from Syracuse, New York, where Dad's carry-on bag went through the screening checkpoint with no problem. Candy is quite legal to bring aboard an airplane, of course. Shampoo or liquids? Probably not; M&M's? No problem. We flew from Syracuse to JFK and then on to Heathrow in London.

In London, before our connecting flight to Italy, we had to go through security again and this time, we did not exactly cruise through easily. Dad was told his bag was going to have to be emptied and checked thoroughly.

He stood there and watched as the female examiner pulled out candy bars ... and bags of caramels ... and other bags of hard candies ... and small boxes of assorted chocolates ... and more candy bars ... and packs of gum and lifesavers ... and ... well, you get the point.

All the while, Dad was carrying on a running conversation with her.

"I don't know what the problem is, this bag was fine in Syracuse," he said. "We had no problem like this in Syracuse. In Syracuse, they let us go right through."

"Well, sir," she would say calmly, "this isn't Syracuse."

And Dad would shake his head and roll his eyes.

Finally, when she had emptied that carry-on of its entire, sweet contents, spread them out on the table and gone through every single piece – and I mean every ... single ... piece – to assure none were explosive devices, she declared: "OK, sir. Thank you. Your bag is fine, you can go."

Then she winked at Dad and said, in a heavy British accent, "I must say, though, for an older bloke, you really have quite the sweet tooth, sir."

Of course, frustrated, Dad could not let that comment pass. He tried to explain that they would be gifts for his friends in Italy, but she'd had enough and casually walked away ... leaving us with the chore of re-stuffing all that candy back into the bag, much to Dad's chagrin. As carefully as he had tried to pack it back at home, now we were quickly slamming everything in haphazardly because we had to rush to catch our next flight. Half the candy bars ended up broken, the caramels were smashed, the hard candies chipped. Dad still passed them out at various relatives' tables, but he had to make sure he told the story of how unreasonable they were in Heathrow, too. You know those Brits, they just don't like Italians!

I could only shake *my* head and roll *my* eyes.

One more airport story, although this one has to do more with

Dad's person than his luggage. It was 2009. We had a group trip going to Tuscany for two weeks; Dad was traveling over with us but was going to spend the two weeks with his brother in San Salvatore Telesino while we were enjoying the Chianti region.

We were at Hancock International Airport in Syracuse for the first leg of our journey and were going through the TSA checkpoint. It happened to be a period of intense scrutiny and high security, so naturally, Dad's carry-on got checked over very closely, as did all of ours. Then, we were instructed to take off all belts, jackets, jewelry and even shoes before we walked through the screening machine. Dad had never been asked to take his shoes off before, and he thought, because of his age, he shouldn't have to.

The TSA agent insisted that yes, he did have to take off his shoes, just like everyone else, to which Dad said – quite loudly enough so that everyone could hear – "Why my shoes? What do you think, that I got a *bomb* in my shoes?!"

He said it half-jokingly, though he really was annoyed.

But if you want to talk about being annoyed, you should have seen the TSA agents, three of which immediately scrambled over to him and surrounded him with stern looks and rigid dispositions. Remember, this was only eight years removed from 9/11 and any mention of bombs – lightheartedly or otherwise – was not appreciated. It still isn't. If you want to see a busy, bustling, noisy airport screening line come to a complete, immediate, slam-bang halt, just try uttering something like that.

Remember the old joke about never yelling "fire" in a crowded movie theater. This was the modern-day version of that.

With all eyes on him, silence all around, and three agents in his face, Dad realized he had said something he maybe, possibly shouldn't have, but it was too late. They whisked him away to a private room where they had him strip down to his underwear while they checked – and re-checked – every article of clothing, every item in his carry-on bag, and every single inch of his body.

Of course, they didn't find anything and eventually let him go, but the withdrawn look on Dad's face as he left that private screening room said it all. To say nothing of the look on his face after his only son – me – got done chewing him out.

"Dad, you do NOT mention the word 'bomb' in an airport. Ever. Not ever. Do you get it?"

That was the scaled down, printable version of what I said, and on the handful of trips we have made since then, I am always sure to remind him, before we leave for the airport, of that lesson.

"No bombs, Dad, got it?"

It wasn't funny at the time, but it has become sort of an inside joke at this point.

Happily, Dad's luggage misfortunes and general airport slipups haven't really rubbed off on me, but I did have a carry-on episode of my own on a trip to Italy in 2017. On the return portion, as I walked through security in Rome, I was stopped because something in my bag had set off an alarm. I couldn't imagine what it might be, but when the examiner went through my possessions, he pulled out a corkscrew and said that was the culprit.

Remember, this was in Italy, though. He looked at his fellow security worker, held up the corkscrew, winked and said something like, "Hey, everyone needs one of these, especially in Italy, no?"

My reason for having it, exactly. He stuffed it back in my carry-on, waved us on, and we were on our way home to America.

I never had another reason to think any more about that corkscrew until we were at JFK and had to go through security *again* before our flight to Syracuse. Again, an alarm went off as the bag went through an X-ray machine, and I was pulled out of line so that a TSA agent could inspect my bag.

She pulled out that corkscrew and gave me a "Tsk, tsk, tsk" sound, wagging her finger at me while saying that she was going to have to confiscate it.

"This could be construed as a weapon, sir. You can't have it in your carry-on. I'm going to have to take it away."

Way too tired to argue or put up any kind of fuss – like my Dad might have – I simply said, "Go ahead, I have dozens more at home."

But I thought to myself, "This is the difference between Italy and the United States. In Italy they realize everyone needs a corkscrew to open a bottle of vino; in the U.S., it's considered a weapon."

Sigh.

Happy trails.

22

An Indestructible Spirit

Finche vi è fiato vi è speranza. – *Old Italian proverb*
Literally: While there's life there's hope.

Earthquakes and Italy really don't mix. Especially those centuries-old towns and villages built in and around the craggy Apennine Mountains that run for 750 miles down the country's spine.

Many of the buildings in those towns are made of concrete, limestone, even stone from volcanic eruptions called *tufa*. They are natural insulators that keep the interior of homes cool in the hot Mediterranean summers and warm during the gray winters.

However, they are far from earthquake resistant, and when the earth rumbles, they crumble like a child's building blocks.

Pictures and videos of those demolished buildings are what we saw from central Italy for a number of months in 2016 when the region was hit twice – first that August by a major 6.2-magnitude earthquake followed by dozens of significant aftershocks, and then in October by a larger 6.6-magnitude tremblor.

It broke my heart in August every time another body was pulled from the wreckage of formerly beautiful hilltop towns such as Amatrice and Accumoli. Amatrice is probably most famous for a spicy pasta dish called *Pasta Amatriciana* and for hosting a famous festival each year to celebrate and pay homage to it; now it was making sad headlines for another reason.

In the October event, miraculously, no one died, but it again touched me every time I watched footage or photos from the historic and formerly lovely towns of Norcia and Visso.

I have visited that gorgeous region – noted for its great food and wine and its uber-friendly people – a handful of times, but the earthquake coverage was even more personal because those quakes reminded me of my own Dad's brush with a *terremoto* some 36 years earlier.

It was 1980, and Dad went home to the southern Campania region for his mother's funeral, my *nonna* Teresa Ereditario Cutillo. The sadness of that occasion was intensified just a few days after she was buried when an even more staggering 7.1-magnitude earthquake rocked the region. The epicenter of that quake was only 68 miles from Dad's village in a town called Conza; nearly 2,500 people died, 7,700 people were injured and an astonishing 250,000 were left homeless.

San Salvatore Telesino certainly wasn't wiped out but several homes and buildings crumbled or were badly damaged – just like they were in Umbria and Lazio in more recent years. In fact, Dad was at a friend's farmhouse when the quake struck, and he was the last one out of the stone home before it collapsed to the ground, the back of his legs scraped up a bit by falling debris. That's how close he came to being trapped under maybe hundreds – probably thousands – of pounds of rubble and stone. Dad had never been in a full-fledged earthquake before, though he'd felt a few rumblings over the years. He said, however, that almost the moment it started happening – initiated by the lights and electricity flashing and then going off – everyone knew immediately what was occurring.

Some of the dead in the count of 2,500 were from his village, some were friends. Those who survived didn't dare return to their homes. They spent the next week or so sleeping under the stars in open fields where there was no danger of anything falling on them as the aftershocks continued to shake the area – and the nerves. Dad remembers fondly how the folks all bonded out in those fields, how they cooked together, drank wine and sang songs to pass the time. Some of them remain among his dearest friends – they weren't necessarily close before the earthquake, but those friendships made and cemented are a testament to the spirit and camaraderie that can develop in dark, trying times.

This also was long before cell phones, Skype, Facebook and even computers, really, so as difficult as it was on Dad, it was perhaps even more so for us back in the United States, trying desperately to get information. I was a sophomore at St. John Fisher College in Rochester, New York, getting ready to go home for Thanksgiving break when my Mom called me on Sunday asking if I'd seen the evening news, which I hadn't. She told me they were reporting the earthquake, and all she could tell, from the rudimentary graphics, was that it looked like it had happened in the general area of Dad's village. All communication lines in southern Italy were down so there was no way to know if Dad was, indeed, in the middle of it, or even if he were dead or alive. Mom's brother, my Uncle Valentino, even called the White House to inquire if there was any way that someone there could get a list of the dead from Italy. Our local newspaper wrote about Uncle Val's efforts but none of it did any good. We received no word from or about Dad.

He was due back on Thanksgiving Day, which was Thursday, Nov. 27 in 1980. It wasn't until that day – when Mom called the airline and learned that a Michael Cutillo had indeed checked on for the overseas flight from Rome to New York City – that we began to breathe a little bit more normally. It got even better later when we learned Michael Cutillo also was on the connecting flight from New York to Syracuse.

After Dad stepped off the plane in Syracuse, still haggard and unshaven from many days living in the fields with his friends, new and old, and we had welcomed him home with tight, emotional embraces, we went on to have the most memorable Thanksgiving celebration of our lives.

Dad told us that the only reason he had been able to get back to us on time was because his brother, my Zio Enzo, was a well-respected military man in the Italian Army, a colonel at the time. Many roads were still very much impassable the day Dad was scheduled to fly home, and the general public was prohibited from driving on them. However, my uncle was able to use his credentials to drive his brother to the Naples airport and get him started on his way back to America.

So those are the emotions that I relived as I watched those 2016 earthquake recovery efforts unfold in central Italy. I also knew, without a doubt, that the folks in Umbria and all those small towns and villages would rebound and rebuild — my Dad's region sure did. While their homes, churches and hospitals may have been shattered, their indominable spirit never would be.

23

Italian Street Madness

Il riso fa buon sangue. – *Traditional Italian saying*

Literally: Laughter makes good blood.

English equivalent: Laughter is the best medicine.

Yes, sometimes, you just have to laugh, and in Italy, if you don't laugh when it comes to driving, you probably will scream.

I smile and nod politely when people tell me how difficult it is to drive in New York City, especially Manhattan. If you've ever driven in Italy, the Big Apple is a piece of *panettone* ... er, cake.

New York City, with its grid pattern, is one of the easier big cities to navigate, I think. Up one street, down another. Sure, there can be bumper-to-bumper traffic and you need to be aware of one-way signs, honking cab and Uber drivers, pedestrians and messengers on bicycles, but they're just nuisances. They may slow your trip, but they won't throw it all off course.

Navigating cities in Italy – cities that are 2,000 or more years old, by the way, and were built for donkey traffic not Volkswagens, Saabs and Fiats – is a whole different story. Grid? Are you kidding? Gridlock maybe but no grid. No Italian city is set up with parallel street construction.

The Italian word for street corner – or "corn" as Dad would say in his broken English, as you know by now – is *angolo*, which literally means angle. That's about right because every corner in the Old Country is some kind of an angle, and none of them are 90 degrees. OK, maybe I'm exaggerating, but you get the point.

Milan may be the closest thing to a city of somewhat straight, somewhat parallel-running streets, being one of the more modern layouts. But even there, you run into different kinds of trouble, most notably specific lanes for specific vehicles. If you end up in the bus lane when you're driving anything other than a bus, whew do I feel sorry for you. It's impossible to get out of that lane because in Milan they separate those various lanes not by painted lines on the street but by curbs. When you're in the wrong lane, you are *really* in the wrong lane, and you are in it for good – or at least until you get to the next open intersection. And naturally, being in the wrong lane causes some kind of affliction in the offended bus drivers behind you who act like you have put a curse on their entire families.

Not like that's ever happened to me. Much.

Another thing that makes Italy so difficult to navigate for a non-native is the way street names are marked – or not marked. In the busy *centro* areas of most cities, there are no signposts with green street signs like we're used to in America. Many of the names of streets are on plates embedded into the buildings themselves at a certain height, and if you don't know precisely where to look for them, they happen to be quite easy to miss.

A logical question follows: Should you slow down to crane your neck to look for one of those street signs? Let's just say you *don't want* to slow down to crane your neck to look for one of those streets signs and leave it at that. OK, *paisan?*

I also discovered that the names of those streets can change. Often.

We were in Padua once – *Padova* to the *italiani* – beautiful religious, artistic and historic city up north in the Veneto region. I was going to walk from our hotel – I didn't dare drive – to the railroad station to meet my sister Lisa and her husband who were coming in by train from Roma. I asked the very nice man at the front desk of the hotel how I could get *a piedi* – by walking – to the *stazione,* and he told me very politely in what I thought was excellent detail.

It was about a half-mile walk, he said, as he recited, very specifically and seemingly helpfully, all the names of the streets I needed to take to get there. It sounded like a bunch of streets, so I asked him to write them down, which he, again, very pleasantly did. Then I asked him if he had a map, and he did, again graciously unfolding one for me. I wanted to see for myself what I was getting into. What I learned when I looked at the map made me smile. It basically was a straight shot to the railroad station, one long street that simply changed names a number of times. Via del Santo became Via Zaberella became Piazza Eremitani became Corso Garibaldi. That sort of thing. It seems like the Italians have so many people to name streets after with their long and glorious history, but only so many streets, so they use a bunch of names on each one.

That's my quite uneducated guess, anyway.

As the years went on and technology improved, I often wondered what it would be like to drive a car in Italy with a Global Positioning System – better known as a GPS. Obviously, one doesn't need maps so much any more as long as there is a GPS either in the car or on your phone.

Two quick stories about that …

My Dad and I made a family trip in 2016, no real sightseeing or anything like that, just visiting friends and relatives. Sadly, it turned out to be the last time that he would see his brother, my Zio Enzo, before zio died. We rented a car at the Naples airport when we arrived, and our first stop was going to be the city of Caserta, where Zio Enzo and Zia Rita lived in a condo downtown, on Viale Lincoln – yes, named after our great American President.

I'd been there numerous times but always had trouble because Viale Lincoln has sections that, get this, are one-way going east, other sections that are one-way going west, and completely other sections that are two-way going east *and* west – hmmm, come to think of it, that could be a whole chapter on its own! My uncle's place was on a block with one-way traffic going west, and of course, as fate would have it, I always seemed to get to that block via a two-way portion but going east – in other words, *against* traffic for zio's place – which is what happened this day. My problem was compounded by the fact that Dad cannot walk long distances anymore and needed me to park the car basically right in front of my uncle's condo; six inches would be about right; 12 inches? Uh, too far away. You can guess the probability of finding such a space in a bustling Italian city.

What I had to do was drive on a nearby street, not parallel because there are no parallel streets in Italy as I've noted, but one that was heading in the general east-west direction, and go far enough east so that I could take a connecting side street up to Viale Lincoln and then drive west to my uncle's place.

Simple, right? Are you getting a headache reading all that? I sure did while I was driving it.

Oh, did I mention that Dad, in addition to not being able to walk, was not a very good navigator either? He kept saying things like, "This city has changed a lot since I used to come here … like that building, it never used to be there." I kept telling him it really didn't do me any good whatsoever to know what the city *used* to look like. I needed to know how to get to my uncle's place *today*.

So, I turned to my cellphone and its built-in GPS. Turn it on, and it is an infinitely better navigator than Dad, but the dilemma was that I obviously was not connected to Wi-Fi and my phone – with the GPS running – was gobbling up oodles of data. It took about an hour to navigate our way around, and my phone was online the entire time, consuming data like a ravenous animal. What I eventually ended up doing was finding a public lot that was a few blocks from my uncle's condo, parking the car and calling my cousin Anna's husband Angelo. I asked him to come and pick us up, which he said he would do with no problem. We waited a bit for Angelo and then had to ride a little to get to my uncle's place. The entire trip, from the Naples airport to the time we got to my uncle's was about three hours, and I had my phone connected to the internet almost the entire time!

Can you say, *arrivederci* data?

I received a text from my provider telling me that I had used up all my allotted data and that anything I used from that point forward was going to cost me something like $1 million a second. OK, I'm exaggerating, but remember, my friends, this was on the VERY FIRST DAY of our 10-day vacation. First day, data gone. *Se ne va*, as they say in Italian.

Because my wife was on the same data and phone plan as me, she also received that notice on her phone back in America, and of course, immediately wondered what her dumb husband was up to. How could he have used all that data the very first day?

I called her after we settled in and told her in a quick – *very* quick – conversation what the issue had been. I also told her I wouldn't be contacting her often for the rest of the trip. I used my phone very little the rest of the way on that sojourn, but we still ended up with a $500 bill!

I figure I probably could have taken a taxi from the airport to my uncle's place in Caserta – and back again! – for less than $500, but that's what it cost me because I decided to use my phone to help me find my way.

Ouch. And lesson learned.

I also always wondered how modern technology such as GPS would handle Italy's very ancient layout with its small, narrow streets, many of which aren't any larger than alleyways. I got my answer to that during a 2015 trip with my daughter Kristine.

We had visited the Abbey at Montecassino and afterward were heading north to Zagarolo, a small town east of Rome where my cousin Pierluigi Cutillo is chief of police. I had Kristine set the GPS in our rented Fiat for Pigi's address, and she instructed the GPS to use "The Most Direct Route" – or something like that – to get us there.

First, we had to get down off the mountain and through the city of Cassino and then onto a highway that would lead us to Zagarolo. It was that "through the city of Cassino" part that had made this trip memorable.

While we figured The Most Direct Route would take us on main roads and highways – and it eventually did – where the GPS led us while we were within city limits was over some of those small, narrow, snarly streets that were more like alleyways. Our Fiat was small, but these roads, if you could call them that, were not made for automobiles of any sort. They were made for carts full of zucchini, I surmised, but when you looked at them on the GPS-provided map, they were indeed *the most direct route* to the highway.

We turned down one street – as instructed by our friendly GPS voice – and I swear it was an alleyway. There was no way that two cars would be able to pass each other. I really thought that perhaps it was one-way, and I had just missed the sign telling us so. It was obviously a residential neighborhood just on the edge of the city, and it seemed like all the properties had gardens filled with ripe produce. It was a hilly little neighborhood and all those homes also had stone retaining walls as we made our way down the street.

At the end of the straightaway, the road turned sharply to the right, and there was one of those curved convex traffic mirrors stationed at the curve. They are meant to help drivers as you can see your half of the road in the left side of the mirror and the other side – or blind side – on the right side of it.

We were tooling along slowly but nicely when I glanced up at that mirror from a distance and saw that there was another Fiat coming toward us. Maybe this isn't a one-way street, I thought to myself, and maybe two cars really can squeeze by each other. At the very least we were going to find out.

The answer: No, they can't.

As I got to that bend, so did the other car. We both stopped, and there we were, nose to nose, neither able to go another centimeter. The woman driver in the other car started gesturing frenetically with hand motions that were signaling me to back up. I, at first, just shrugged my shoulders because I was afraid to back up with the car squeezed by stone retaining walls on either side. She continued cursing at me like I remembered those bus drivers in Milan doing, but another thing I had to take into consideration was that I was driving a 5-speed standard shift vehicle.

If you've driven a standard, you know that you need to press the clutch to the floor with your left foot in order to engage the gears. You also know that when you are on a hill, as we were, and you press that clutch, the car is going to roll forward before you are able to give it enough gas to get it moving backward.

The distance, again, between our two cars? Inches.

I knew that if I pushed in the clutch, even if only for a second, my car would roll into hers. Can you say, "Who's your insurance carrier?" in Italian.

So instead, I started motioning for her to move back. I just wanted her to back up a tad to give me some room, but my hand gestures apparently didn't translate. She must have thought I was signaling her to move into the bus lane in Milan or something.

And that led her to signal even more vehemently for *me* to move back.

We both were waving expressively, and this whole scene really should have been set to music, some kind of symphony, like Wolfgang Amadeus Mozart's No. 22 in C Major.

Finally, with neither of us going anywhere fast, I told my daughter to hang on because I was just going to gun it in reverse, hoping that I could keep the steering wheel straight enough so that the rental car would not veer off and scrape against any of those retaining walls.

So, with the stick shift in reverse, I pushed the clutch in ever so slightly, rolled just a tad forward and laid on the gas so hard that we shot backward like a rocket. Back, back, back we went – staying on the street the whole way. We may have wobbled but we never scraped; no retaining walls were rubbed against. I drove back in reverse almost up to the top of the street/alleyway before putting on the brakes.

The woman then very casually was able to drive up toward us but only to the very first property where she turned right, into the driveway. Without a thank-you wave or any kind of acknowledgement of my all-star daring backward maneuvering (and yes, thank God, there were no cars behind me). I figured that if that property really was where the woman lived, she probably had to battle this kind of scenario daily and had grown used to and/or tired of it. I don't know, but I didn't need to find out. We had an appointment in Zagarolo.

When her heart lowered from her throat, Kristine looked at me and said, "Nice work, Dad."

I said, "Thanks … and can you turn that GPS off?"

Still, I think my all-time favorite story about navigating Italian streets was pre-GPS days and again goes back to the ancient city of Padua. We were on a one-way street looking for our hotel across the way from the famed St. Anthony's basilica. We were sort of creeping along very carefully, but we noticed we had passed the hotel where we had reservations. I hit the brakes when I realized that, and Dad encouraged me to back up the few hundred feet back to our hotel; yes, against the traffic if you're following along. I just couldn't bring myself to do that, but there was a corner not that far ahead. I figured I would take a right at the corner, take another right and another right – basically going around the block – and get back to the one-way street again.

Hah!

City blocks in Italy aren't like blocks in America. They aren't like blocks anywhere. In fact, I dare say that they aren't blocks at all. They're more like wacky jigsaw puzzle pieces, with no symmetry to them at all, especially grid-like symmetry such as we are used to.

I took that first right, alright, but then we just went straight … and straight some more, and then we kind of veered left. There *was* no other right, but we passed a left turn and then another left turn. I kept on driving straight, hoping for a right, but we passed another left turn and another. I don't know how far we went exactly, but we eventually pulled up to the end of the street we were on and – guess what? – we could only go left. So, I did. Then, after various other lefts and rights, and a few near collisions with vespa drivers and touristic horse-and-buggies, we were completely lost. The buildings of this historic city weren't particularly high, but they were so close to the street that there was no frame of reference, nothing for me to look at and say, "Oh yeah, I need to get over there by that church."

It ended up taking us two hours to get back to the hotel. Let me put this another way: TWO HOURS!!!! Because I took one right turn. We stopped at one gas station – the same gas station – so many times and became so familiar I thought they were going to invite us for Christmas dinner. The first time we asked for directions, the attendant very cordially told us what we needed to do, though he said it so rapidly that I only caught the first two – of probably about 15 – turns that I needed to make. The second time we stopped there, he recognized us and laughed. The third time, we recognized him and laughed. Though we wanted to cry.

We eventually made it, and that is when I had to ask the man at the hotel directions to walk to the train station to meet my sister.

Speaking of laughing, that's really all you can do when driving around Italy – hence the proverb that tops this chapter. Keep your sense of humor ... and a map, or a GPS system, right by your side. And if you're using your phone, make sure you have lots of data set aside.

24

Ensuring That We
Never Forget

I fratelli uniti tra loro formano un fascio che pùo resistere agli sforzi più robusti. – *Traditional saying*

Literally: Brothers joined together form a bundle that can withstand the toughest efforts.

English equivalent: United we stand, divided we fall; union is strength.

My cousin Claudio Gentile, 13 years old at the time, was leaning absolutely as far out the passenger side window as he possibly could while still officially being "inside" our car. I thought he was going to crack a vertebra or something as he craned to look up at all the tall buildings. Either that, or he was going to get clipped by a passing yellow cab or messenger on a bicycle.

Skyscrapers – *grattacieli*, one of my favorite Italian words that literally means "scratching the sky" – had caught Claudio's youthful eye.

We were cruising the main streets of Manhattan. My father was in the back seat. I was driving. Claudio was marveling at New York City's glistening grandeur on a picture-postcard, blue-sky afternoon.

It was 1998.

"*Ah, finalmente,*" Claudio was declaring. "*Questa è l'america. Alla fine ho visto l'America.*" Finally, this is America. At long last, I have seen America!!

My father answered from the rear seat behind us.

"*No, no, Claudio. Questa non è l'america. L'america è dove abita la nostra famiglia, Syracuse. Questo è solamente un sacco di edifici alti.*" No, Claudio, this is not America. America is where our family lives, Syracuse. This is just a lot of tall buildings.

Dad was not disparaging the Big Apple, by any means, and he realizes that millions of people call New York City home, but his point was simply that old saying, "Home is where the heart is." The Italians have an expression for that, too (of course, right?): *La famiglia è la patria del cuore.* For Dad, his heart is not in NYC but back where the family lived, where we grew our tomatoes, where we celebrated birthdays, where we hung our capicola near the basement window so the breeze could dry it out. Claudio's point, on the other hand, was that the symbol of the United States of America for so many people around the globe is New York City with its mighty buildings and recognizable, familiar sites.

Anyway, block by Manhattan block, the debate raged on. I listened as I navigated Broadway and Wall Street, Fifth Avenue and Mulberry Street. And somehow, I knew what both my passengers meant.

Claudio had spent a month with *la famiglia* in Syracuse and Upstate New York and sure, it was fantastic visiting the American side of his family for the first time in the United States. He went to a different home almost every night for dinner, visiting relatives he didn't even know existed.

That was great and that was the America Dad wanted to show his brother's only grandchild. It was the America Dad knew, the American dream he had built since making the life-altering decision to marry Mom and come to the United States in 1958.

But to the young Italian boy – in fact, to millions of young foreign boys and girls – mention America and what comes to mind? Not Uncle Louie's place in Fulton or Uncle Sandy's nicely-appointed house in suburbia. Chances are, it's New York City with the Statue of Liberty ... the hustle and bustle and neon lights ... the museums and theaters ... the Yankees, Mets and Knicks ... and yes, those skyscrapers, those *grattacieli*.

So, the day before we were going to put Claudio on a flight to go back home to Italy, we took him to New York City to see those sights and experience the glitz for which he had been longing.

"*Finalmente,*" he said again, gazing upward, always upward. "*Questa è l'America, la vera America. La bella America.*" Finally, this is America, the real America, America the Beautiful!

He even uttered it in English with an Italian accent, saying, "Be-uuuu-TEE-ful."

Dad just shook his head. He didn't feel like continuing the argument any longer, though. He may have understood Claudio's point, he may not have. Maybe he had a headache or possibly was just catching a cat nap, I wasn't sure. As we continued our tour, Claudio took photo after photo – of Times Square, Madison Square Garden, Grand Central Station, the United Nations. All those quintessential New York City sites.

Then we came upon maybe the most representative, if not the most glorious, symbol of America's grandeur, at least to Claudio ... the World Trade Center. The Twin Towers.

His eyes looked like a couple of giant olives bugging out of their sockets. His mouth hung open in awe as he looked up ... up ... and even further up. It's something I never will forget, seeing – through my cousin's eyes, those windows to the soul – how those wondrous structures moved and astonished him.

It was the quietest that he had been during our entire back-bending, horn-honking, debate-holding tour of New York City, and after a few moments that seemed like Roman centuries, he uttered, this time in a reverent tone, just one word: "America" ... or as the Italians say it, "*AH ... mer ... EE ... cuh.*"

We got out of the car to gaze up at those two beauties, and even as dozens – maybe hundreds – of New Yorkers rushed by us on their appointed rounds, it seemed like we were the only three people there. We went inside to take the elevator to the observation deck of the south tower from where Claudio, in continued amazement, said he thought he could see all the way to Italy.

"What's your father doing," I jokingly asked. "*Cosa sta facendo tuo padre?*"

"*Ci sta salutando,*" Claudio laughed. "He's waving at us."

I was 38 at the time, but I think that's the exact moment when I realized more than ever how very special America is, whether you're talking about her people, her families, as Dad had been – in upstate New York, New York City, Kansas, Walla Walla, Washington, or wherever. Or whether you're talking about her epochal magnificence as Claudio had been – the Empire State Building, the Golden Gate Bridge, Niagara Falls, the Grand Canyon, Mount Rushmore.

Or the World Trade Center.

Of course, those symbols of American strength and power, while mesmerizing and inspiring to many, also drew the attention and the jealousy of those whose hearts are full of darkness.

We all know what happened to the Twin Towers on Sept. 11, 2001 and we must continue to go to great measures to make sure that we never forget – we must always remember and honor those who were lost in the tragedy; and the heroic first responders, many of whom have died in the intervening years because of diseases contracted while helping others; and those, like my wife's brave son Philip and all the other young men and women, who went off to fight America's enemies that were connected to the cowardly, despicable attack.

I know that Claudio hasn't forgotten, nor have others around the world who watched with us, in horror, as the Towers – symbols of America's power and might – collapsed that day.

In a way, though, while strengthening our own resolve here at home, that episode also drew much of the world closer to us. Now, every time I visit my cousin in Italy, Claudio, a grown man, pulls out his photo album from that 1998 trip. He flips through a few pages until he finds just the right ones – the ones with the shots he took of the World Trade Center that day back when the world seemed so much simpler and so much gentler.

What strikes me is that the sky seems as blue in his pictures as it was on Sept. 11, 2001. He points to the Towers in his photographs and says, again, just the one word: "America."

And I nod my head in agreement with him.

"AH ... mer ... EE ... cuh ... the Be-uuuu-TEE-ful."

VIAGGI IN ITALIA

TRIPS TO ITALY

25

How About A Little Lard To Go With That?

Colonnata, Provincia di Massa-Carrara, Toscana

Tanto va la gatta al lardo che ci lascia lo zampino. – *Old Italian proverb*

Literally: The cat goes to the lard so often that he leaves a paw print there.

What it means: Getting away with something may be possible once but don't do it again because next time you may not be so lucky!

American equivalent: Curiosity killed the cat

You can stare at some Italian words for hours and still not figure out what they mean. You may have run across a few of those words or phrases as you've been perusing the proverbs that jumpstart each chapter in this book. It's understandable with a foreign language.

Lardo, however, is most decidedly not one of those types of words.

We could play that old children's game, and I could say I'd give you three guesses and the first two don't count. But I don't think we would even need to go that far. With *lardo*, what you see is what you get. Or at least, it seems to be.

It's lard. Of course. But there is more to this story.

What you see – or say – is really not quite what you get. Italian *lardo* is not the kind of lard your grandmother Teresa or your Aunt Josephine uses to make flaky pie crust. That's another entirely different word in Italian – *strutto*, which is the type of lard used in frying and dough making.

Lardo is something else all over again, and on one of our group trips, to Tuscany in 2011, it took on a whole new enriching and humorous meaning. Most particularly, the famous *Lardo di Colonnata*. Now, when I say famous, I know there's a pretty good chance that many readers haven't heard of it. In fact, the joke among the locals when our group of Americans tasted this delicacy is that it is famous everywhere in the world ... except in the United States.

As so many places in Italy that are noted for one thing or another, Colonnata, a picturesque ancient village of less than 300 people high in the Apuan Alps near the marble quarries of Carrara, has become known for its lard. Not lard that you cook with, but lard that you eat. No, seriously. That would be *lardo*.

Lardo di Colonnata is cured lard, not unlike cured meat, made from the back fat of select pigs. The pigs are not domesticated and therefore not shot up with hormones and other nasty things but rather can roam and forage and eat natural things such as acorns and chestnuts. It also is said that the gentle mountain breezes in and around Colonnata make the area perfect to raise the type of pig used to make the *lardo*.

The fat is cured with a wonderfully aromatic mixture of fresh spices and herbs, and its production is controlled rigidly by governmental standards, much in the same way that wine production is controlled throughout Italy. Local families guard their generations-old mixture of herb recipes as religiously as others do their wine-making secrets.

The *lardo* is as white as the region's world-famous marble, which when you fly into the Pisa airport is so white that it makes it look like the mountains are always covered with snow, even in the middle of the hottest summer. The tie-in: *Lardo* is cured in special containers chiseled from that local marble, the same marble that was used to build St. Peter's Basilica in Vatican City and from which Michelangelo carved his famous statue of David. Local legend has it that Michelangelo never could have sculpted the statues that he did were it not for the fortification he got from the local *lardo*, of which he grew quite fond while staying and chiseling in the area.

I always say, No. 1, leave it to the Italians to let nothing go to waste, and No. 2, leave it to those same Italians to find a use for everything. *Lardo* fits both rules of thumb very nicely.

It basically developed generations ago when the marble quarrymen – or *cavatori* in Italian – were unable to travel up and down the mountains as easily as they can today. When they worked the quarries they often stayed in one region or area for days, weeks, sometimes months. Food was not so easy to come by, and so they learned to use every bit of an animal, in this case, even the back fat of those local pigs. A slice of *lardo* with onions, tomatoes and extra virgin olive oil between two pieces of crusty, homemade bread, along with a couple of glasses of vino, would give those *cavatori* enough calories and enough energy to work the quarries all day long.

See how it all fits together?

And if consuming back fat from pigs doesn't sound all that appealing, remember, at least – in true Italian resourceful fashion – they made that back fat as palatable as possible with rosemary and thyme and basil and other aromatic and fresh spices. It must be cured for at least six months in the marble containers, after which time the fat has absorbed all the flavors of those herbs.

Even as far back as Roman times, *lardo* was thought to have medicinal properties, and modern-day research has confirmed exactly that. Some studies show that saturated fats can actually increase levels of "good" – or HDL – cholesterol. Other studies show that saturated fat, like that found in *lardo*, can transform LDL – or the "bad" cholesterol – into less harmful forms of LDL cholesterol.

Now, I'm not a doctor, and I certainly am not suggesting a steady diet of the stuff – unless maybe you're mining marble, or *marmo*, in Carrara. However, anything that might actually lower your risk of heart disease? That can't be all-bad, right?

To our group of vacationing Americans, fresh off a marble carving and sculpting demonstration at the *Laboratoria Cava Scuola* in nearby Carrara, a stop at a local *larderia* for a sampling, and an explanation of what it is and how it is made had many feeling like they were on "Bizarre Foods." In fact, the host of that Food Network show, Andrew Zimmern, has indeed sampled *lardo* on an episode or two; I've seen it with my own eyes.

At *Larderia La Stazione*, we were able to taste it with our own mouths. The good folks there were more than happy to show off their best *lardo* to our group, bringing out platter after platter of *crostini* and *bruschette* topped with *lardo* and all sorts of other local charcuterie, including *prosciutto* and *salame*, along with fresh tomatoes and cheese.

While many of the Americans squirmed, especially after learning what had been placed in front of them, the family of Bruna Guadagni, who owned the larderia, stood by the product's tastiness and historic value.

To the locals, it's not a gimmick or a special TV episode; it's a part of life.

To other Italians who can't get the famous *Lardo di Colonnata* that easily, it's a delicacy and a gourmet food item. I even bought some for my Dad who was staying down south at his village on that trip. He was ecstatic to get some because *lardo* was not so easy to come by in San Salvatore Telesino.

Meanwhile, to our group of tourists, it became one of the signature elements of that particular trip to Tuscany. You know, like, "I can barely choke down a glass of Chianti these days unless it's accompanied by some nice fresh *lardo*."

26

When A Duck
Isn't Quite A Duck

Giardini Naxos, Provincia di Messina, Sicilia

Far ridere i polli ... – *Old Italian proverb*

Literally: To make the chickens laugh ...

What it means: If you manage to make the chickens laugh, you've made a fool of yourself, and it's likely you've done something ridiculous!

L'allegria è d'ogni male il rimedio universale. – *Old Italian proverb*

Literally: Happiness is, for everything bad, the best remedy.

What it means: Laughter is the best medicine.

OK, as a duck, I guess I make a good chicken.

There, I've said it. Isn't that the first stage on the road to recovery – admission?

What else can I tell you?

It was the spring of 2007, and I was part of a group of 80 people – two busloads – on a trip that started in Rome and would end up in Palermo, Sicily. We toured the Vatican and the Sistine Chapel, snaked our way down the sun-splashed Amalfi Coast, took a boat ride to the Isle of Capri, stayed two nights at a five-star resort in Vibo Valentia, in the region of Calabria, overlooking the deep blue Mediterranean Sea, and even road on our bus across the Strait of Messina (the bus driving right onto the huge ferry that took us from Reggio Calabria and the mainland of Italy to the island of Sicily). On the island, we would end up in Palermo, the capital city, but on this night – which would turn into The Duck Night, or in Italian *La Serata dell'- Anatra* – we were in Giardini Naxos, the first Greek settlement on Sicily, near Taormina and hard by what is known as the Sicilian Riviera. About half our group was packed comfortably in La Spelonca, a rustic, below-sidewalk-level tavern in the downtown area.

We were enjoying the tavern's *bruschette*, topped with the ripest tomatoes and freshest basil, along with glasses of red (Nero D'Avola) and white (Grillo) wine that were native Sicilian varieties made specifically for La Spelonca, which means The Cavern, by the way.

We also were enjoying the comedy and Sicilian and Neapolitan songs performed by the house band, which included the owner, whose name was Pippo – or at least will be for the purposes of our little story here. Pippo was a jovial, dark-eyebrowed, mustachioed man who obviously had chowed down a few of his restaurant's *bruschette* and *pizze*. His ample stomach made a good resting spot, however, for the acoustic guitar that he played both with gusto and a big smile.

It was noisy and chaotic – just as a Sicilian tavern ought to be – with the waiters and waitresses hustling out the snacks and drinks, Pippo and his band's music and jokes, and the American tourists laughing and recounting the day's journey, which included that ferry ride across the mystical Strait of Messina and then a bus ride up to the ritzy hilltop town of Taormina.

The music that evening included some of the best songs from Naples, such as "Santa Lucia" and "O Sole Mio," along with Sicilian folksongs. Pippo and his crew even lampooned Sicily's reputation as a center for organized crime by playing the love song "Speak Softly Love" to Roger in our group. That tune is much more widely known as the theme of "The Godfather" movies. The band placed a black fedora atop Roger's head, shined a spotlight on him, and kissed his hand as they sang. The rest of us howled with laughter.

For the show's finale, Pippo roamed our crowd and grabbed numerous of us to join him at the front of the room. Notice I said "us." Yes, *amici*, I was now part of The Great Sicilian Floor Show, live from La Spelonca Lounge.

Pippo lined us all up and asked us where we were from so that he could introduce us to the audience. We still did not know what was up. I told him I was from "Napoli." He looked at me, surprised, because he thought I was from America, and asked, "Really?" I said, "No, not really, but my father is."

He then whispered to each one of us what are roles were going to be in what would turn out to be a raucous, rowdy rendition, half in Sicilian, half in English, of "Old McDonald." We had a howling dog, a sexy cat, and even Tarzan for a mighty finish. Yours truly? I was told to be a duck.

A duck, I thought. OK, easy enough. A duck. *Un'anatra*, in Italian. I got this I said to myself. But as the song made its way through that howling dog … and that sexy cat … and got closer to the Italian duck, I realized I didn't really know how to be a duck. Not an Italian one, at least. I didn't know how to quack in Italian, and I didn't really know how to strut or carry on like a duck. I mean, don't they just float on the water?

So, when the spotlight zeroed in on me, I did the only thing that came to mind. Harkening back to a song my Dad used to sing to us when we were little, "*Il Ballo Del Qua Qua*," I started flapping my arms and strutting for all I was worth.

The reaction from my traveling *amici* was quick, sharp and to the point. "What the heck kind of duck is that?" they yelled between laughs. "That's a chicken!"

True enough, "*Il Ballo Del Qua Qua*" is the Italian version of that great American wedding reception tune, "The Chicken Dance."

I looked at Pippo, who didn't miss a strum on his guitar but was laughing as hard as anyone. I gave him the eyes that said, "It's the best I could come up with on short notice." And, not skipping a beat, Pippo, the true, quick-witted showman that he was, bellowed, "That's a NA-POLITANA duck!"

And so, the song went on, all the way to the mighty Tarzan yell by our friend, John, another Napolitano, by the way, that ended it. We laughed, hugged and slapped backs, all the way back to the hotel.

And so, even though my rendition of an Italian duck left something to be desired – and believe me, I am reminded of it often to this day – it still accomplished something my father also always told me to do: Give them something to remember.

27

Keeping A Special Secret

Frosinone, Provincia di Frosinone, Lazio

Acqua in bocca! – *Traditional Italian saying*

Literally: (Keep the) water in your mouth!

What it means: Keep it to yourself.

An example of how to use it: *"È un segreto, acqua in bocca!"*
"It's a secret, keep it to yourself!"

Non sei capace di tenerti un cece in bocca. – *Old Italian saying*

Literally: You're not able to keep a chickpea in your mouth.

What it means: You can't keep your mouth shut.

An example of how to use it: *"Non dirgli niente, non si sa tenere un cece in bocca!"*
"Don't tell him anything, he's not able to keep his mouth shut"

Wow, talk about almost ruining the surprise…

For Christmas, in 2007, I ordered Jan a copy of the ship's manifest from the trip her paternal grandfather, Pietro Mastracci, made to America in 1906 aboard the Nord America. I tracked it down on the Ellis Island website, and when it arrived, I immediately put it in a beautiful cherry frame and wrapped it up in case she came across it before Natale. And believe me, for a notorious last-minute Christmas shopper, this was no small feat to have pulled off more than a month before Dec. 25.

Knowing that family history means a lot to Jan, though, I figured this special surprise gift – something she neither had asked for nor would have expected – was going to steal the show from all the other presents under the tree that year.

Then, I almost blew it. Having a surprise like that a full month before unveiling it is too much for someone with loose lips like me. We were sitting around on Thanksgiving with the family, talking to my Dad, who, as you know by now, was from the small southern farming village of San Salvatore Telesino.

Now, it's amazing the amount of history that you can learn from just one line about a person on those manifests, and I had looked it over and learned so much about her grandfather before I wrapped it. In fact, I knew things about Pietro that Jan didn't even know, most notably that his hometown – or at least the last town he lived in before coming to America – was Frosinone.

Frosinone is in the Lazio region of Italy, in the mountains about 45 miles south of Rome. A neat thing about it for me is that every time I had driven the A1 *autostrada* – or super highway – to go to San Salvatore Telesino, I passed the exit for Frosinone. I knew exactly where it was.

So, after polishing off our Thanksgiving meal and while eating a piece of *cuccuzz* pie – a dialect word for squash and Dad's word for pumpkin – I asked him, "Hey, Dad, have you ever been to Frosinone?"

"No," he replied. "I know where it is, but I've never been there. Why?"

"Well," I said, all Mr. Know-It-All and everything, "that's where Jan's grandfather is from."

She shot me a look that said, "Where did you ever come up with that bit of information?" Though what came out of her mouth was, "Frosinone? I never heard of that. I always thought he was from Rome."

Just a couple of weeks earlier, she had shown me the papers from when her *nonno* had become a naturalized citizen of the United States, and on those papers, it was stated that Pietro Mastracci was, indeed, from Rome. I knew what it said because I saw the papers, but after checking out the manifest – with his hometown listed as

Frosinone – I figured the naturalization papers were probably just estimating the region from which he hailed. The world-famous city of Rome is easier to tell someone filling out papers than little-known Frosinone.

"No," I said. "He was from Frosinone. It says so right on the ..."

Whoa, I slammed on the brakes. Thankfully, I caught myself, realizing that the conversation was going down an avenue that I didn't want it to go down until Dec. 25. This called for some quick thinking as the room fell about as quiet as Sunday Mass.

"Right on the ... *what?*" she asked.

Jan realizes that I know a lot about the Old Country, and so she'll defer to my knowledge of it most of the time. I knew this. So, I used it. I said something about there really were very few immigrants who came over from Rome, most came from the poorer regions further south, and I told her that I read something somewhere that explained that most of those who were said to have come from Rome were really from a town called Frosinone, south of Rome. "So, chances were good, you see, that your grandfather Pietro was from Frosinone, not Rome proper."

I lied, in other words. Big time. Then I waited ...

And waited ...

And finally ... she bought it.

Then I quickly asked for another piece of *cuccuzz* pie to change the subject.

Whew.

And so, her family history was not brought up again until Christmas Day when she unwrapped the gift and was as stunned and as thrilled as I'd hoped she would be.

Now, back to that manifest itself and what it taught us. We learned that Pietro Mastracci was 23 years old and single when he came to America. He was a laborer who was healthy and whose ticket had been purchased by his brother, Filippo. He was not a polygamist, which I thought was nice. He had all of $15 in his pocket, which maybe wasn't so nice, and after he arrived in New York City on March 15, 1906, his brother was going to be taking him north up to a little village called Lyons, New York, between Rochester and Syracuse, and they were going to live at 17 Canal St.

Jan didn't know any of that. She knew that her grandfather adored her. And that he loved playing Italian card games with her. And that he would tease her, claiming she cheated by saying, in broken English, "*You cheap me, Gianetta, you cheap me.*" Oh yeah, and she knew that he taught her Italian songs like "*Poco Pane,*" the words to which she remembers to this day.

That's what she knew about Pietro Mastracci. She certainly did not know that he originally came from the mountains south of Rome, a town called Frosinone. Not until she read it on the manifest from Ellis Island.

Thank God, I managed to keep that a secret, even with my big mouth. Talk about almost spilling the chi chi beans.

Fast forward to June 2011 when Jan and I were on one of my group trips, this one to the Amalfi Coast. We broke off from the group for a few days, rented a car and first visited my Dad's village for a day and then cruised further north to check out the bustling city that once was home to Pietro Mastracci.

Frosinone – pronounced fro-zee-NO-nay – has a population of about 46,000, and traces of the settlement go back 4,000 years. Once home to groups such as the Samnites, it was destroyed several times by foreign invaders. After the sack of Rome in 1527, the Germans, Florentines, French and Spanish took turns ravaging it. During World War II, because of its proximity to Rome, it was bombed over 50 times, and the first Allied troops entered the city on May 31, 1944.

The Province of Frosinone, of which the city was made the capital in 1927 by the Fascist government, includes Mount Ernici and Mount Ausoni and the Liri and Sacco valleys, which lead to the Gulf of Gaeta on the Mediterranean Sea.

Tourists don't exactly flock to Frosinone, probably because it gets lost in the shuffle that is Rome just to the north and the famous Abbey at Montecassino 40 miles to the south. However, the area does have a handful of ski resorts, because of those mountains, and hot springs, a famous folk festival, and in Fiuggi, the *"Festa delle Stuzze,"* when a large fire is built dedicated to patron Saint Biagio.

At times over the years – including in 2018-19 – Frosinone also has had a soccer team that played in Italy's top league, *Serie A*, making it a "major league" city for those seasons. The squad, nicknamed the Canaries, was founded in 1912 and plays in 16,000-seat Stadio Benito Stirpe.

According to genealogy websites, the most common surnames in Frosinone include Carnevale, DeSantis, Evangelista, Fiorini, Rossi and Valente, but Jan and I were in search of anyone named Mastracci.

When we pulled into the historic city hall, it was late on a Friday afternoon, probably the absolute worst time to begin any major genealogical sleuthing – in Italy or anywhere else for that matter. The folks in the office, though pleasant, were already looking forward to their weekend and really didn't want to yank out all kinds of records for the two Americans in search of family history. One woman, however, did open a phone book for us, and we were delighted to see that there were six Mastracci families listed. We wrote down the phone numbers, thanked the folks for their help, wished them *"un buon weekend,"* and immediately went to find a little trattoria for lunch; this family history-searching thing really builds an appetite!

After *pranzo*, we scored a nice little three-star hotel, which was painted orange like my favorite college basketball team, Syracuse University – a good sign, I thought. It also was on a street named after Licinio Refice, who I had not heard of but a quick look on Wikipedia showed he was a composer and a *priest*! Now that, I thought, was an interesting combination, perhaps found only in Italia. We spent the evening relaxing on our orange balcony, talking about Jan's grandpa and enjoying a beautiful bottle of the famous white wine from Frascati, a nearby town in the Roman hills. We also talked about how we would spend the next day, beginning by calling all those six families that were listed in the phone book.

We didn't really know what we expected by doing that, but it's just another one of those adventures that I always enjoy. So, over our morning cappuccinos, I called all six and ventured to explain, in my best

Italian, that we were in town searching for relatives of my wife's grandfather. The tally: Three said they had no relatives who went to America, two did not answer, and one nice young man said he would do more research and get back to me. We exchanged contact information, and I fully expected that I would hear from him again sometime.

I never have.

Oh well.

After breakfast, Jan and I took another ride into the city center to walk for a bit and take some photos. It really was a busy town with some beautiful views of the surrounding hills and valleys. We didn't talk much because Jan was simply soaking it all in, walking the same sidewalks on which her grandfather once walked, past cafes where he undoubtedly must have stopped for an espresso and to chat with his *paisani*. I asked her once what she was thinking about, and she looked at me with tears in her eyes and said, "You know…"

It was only after we drove out of Frosinone and headed south to reunite with our group on Mount Vesuvius that Jan looked at me and said, "I could feel him."

She says that he always has been her Guardian Angel and visiting the city where he lived over 100 years ago really allowed her to connect with him once more. I'm sure she could hear him singing *"Poco Pane."*

Yes, it's amazing what a ship's manifest from Ellis Island can do and the secrets it can reveal.

28

A 'Heavenly' Meal in Saint Pio's Hometown

Pietrelcina, Provincia di Benevento, Campania

Dove non c'è obbedienza non c'è virtù; dove non c'è virtù non c'è amore; dove non c'è amore non c'è Dio, e senza Dio non si và in paradiso.
– *San Pio da Pietrelcina*

Translation: Where there is no obedience there is no virtue; where there is no virtue there is no love; where there is no love there is no God, and without God we do not go to heaven.

Pietrelcina is a pretty little village of neat, cobblestone streets and lovely pastel-colored buildings, at least in the newer part of town. If you know Italy and you saw photos of it, you might guess that it is in Tuscany or Umbria, maybe even a coastal town somewhere in Liguria. But it actually is in Campania, the poorer southern region that claims Naples as its capital. Pietrelcina – pronounced "pee-eh-trell-CHEE-na" – resides in the hills north of the small city of Benevento. It's an area decidedly less famous than Tuscany or Umbria, though Benevento does happen to be known for that delectable, neon-yellow liqueur called Strega that you've read about in previous chapters.

Pietrelcina is about 25 miles east of San Salvatore Telesino and would be about as famous as Dad's village – that is to say, not very much at all – if not for the fact that a boy named Francesco Forgione was born there on May 25, 1887.

The home where Padre Pio was born in the historic section of Pietrelcina.

I joke that the people who live in Pietrelcina – all 3,100 or so – should thank God every single night before they go to bed that He decided Francesco Forgione should be born there. Better yet, they could even thank Francesco himself directly through their prayers because, you see, Francesco Forgione is better known to you and to me – and to just about everyone else in at least the Roman Catholic world – as Padre Pio, who was canonized as a saint by Pope John Paul II in 2002.

Because Padre Pio was born in Pietrelcina, pilgrims flock there by the hundreds of thousands, primarily to the historic part of town to see the centuries-old house where he grew up, including the bed he was laying in when it is said he was visited by Mother Mary, the houses where his parents grew up, and the little neighborhood church, the Church of St. Ann, where he was baptized and made his First Communion and his Confirmation.

Also, just outside of town, there is a plot of land where young Francesco's parents, simple farmers, grew their vegetables; it was there, in the middle of a grove of pine trees, that he is said to have received the stigmata for the very first time of many.

In other words, it was in that grove of pine trees where Pietrelcina struck it rich.

All those pilgrims and all those tourists, who otherwise would avoid this village as much as they avoid San Salvatore Telesino, spend money. Lots of money. Enough money to allow for those beautifully manicured cobblestone streets in the new part of town, along with sparkling, white-marble churches, even a small museum with Padre Pio artifacts, including gloves he wore to hide the wounds of his mysterious stigmata, also known as the Holy Wounds of Christ. A person who receives the stigmata suffers bodily marks and bleeding in spots corresponding to the crucifixion wounds of Jesus. The unexplainable wounds, which healed but reappeared numerous times throughout Padre Pio's life, were said to be a sign of his holiness.

Padre Pio also is said to have had myriad other incredible spiritual gifts, including levitation, mysticism, bilocation – being in two distinct

Antonio DiNunzio carves up a roasted veal shank at his restaurant in Pietrelcina.

locations at the same time – prophecy and the gift of tongues. One story says that in 1947, he heard the confession of a young Polish priest named Karol Józef Wojtyła and told him that one day he would ascend to become the head of the Roman Catholic Church. That young man later became known as Pope John Paul II, the very pope who canonized Padre Pio 43 years after his death.

All that is to say that the renowned little village that was the hometown of Padre Pio is worth a few hours of your time if you ever are in that part of Italy. I have visited a number of times and always enjoy it. I never got to see Padre Pio, who died in 1968, but my Mom and Dad went to a Mass that he said in the larger town of San Giovanni Rotondo, in Puglia near the Adriatic Sea. He spent most of his adult life – from 1916 to 1968 – preaching, performing miracles, and healing the ill in San Giovanni Rotondo. It is said that, while he was ministering in San Giovanni Rotondo, he was asked if he would ever return to Pietrelcina, and he said that he would, but it wouldn't be until after his death.

Over the years of visiting Padre Pio's hometown and bringing friends and relatives there, I even have made a friend who I enjoy seeing almost as much as I would have enjoyed meeting the great Saint Pio. His name is Antonio DiNunzio, and he owns a restaurant in Pietrelcina called *Il Cenacolo*, which translates to "The Last Supper" – quite by design, I'm sure, for a town with a religious artifact or a stigmata glove around every corner.

Every time I go to Pietrelcina, creature of habit that I am, I stop at Antonio's place for *pranzo*, though honestly – because those visits are separated by years – I am not quite sure he remembers me each time. To help jumpstart his memory, I always tell him that I make sure I stop in to see him and that I consider him just like family.

Then he invariably proceeds to feed me and whoever I happen to be traveling with like family, usually going well off the menu with whatever he's got bubbling and cooking and roasting back in the kitchen.

In 2010, I brought Dad and my buddy from Geneva, New York, Steve Venuti, to visit Antonio. After the usual pleasantries, the hugs, the back slaps – again, whether Antonio recognized me or not doesn't matter – he went about the very serious business of feeding us lunch.

We were the only diners at the time because we happened to pop in after the lunch crowd had eaten and departed. Antonio and staff had been getting ready to close up for their afternoon *siesta* but remained open to feed us, so long, he said, as we were content with whatever he could come up with. Were we ever!

He started off this particular "Last Supper" with a most reverent appetizer that included two pieces of roasted pecorino cheese with black truffle shavings in the middle and topped by peppery arugula greens. If I said it was heavenly, being served such a dish in Padre Pio's town, you'd groan, so I won't. Next up was a second saintly appetizer, a little dish of fresh, creamy ricotta cheese drizzled with honey and fruit preserves.

The most pious pasta dish – because every Italian meal *must* have a pasta dish ... or three – was fusilli with fresh tomatoes and porcini mushrooms. The main course that day was an angelic roasted veal shank the size of a baby dinosaur that Antonio himself carved for us at the table. I had to wonder, for only a fleeting moment, how he just happened to have a roasted veal shank back in that mystical kitchen of his, but allowing for the fact that we were, after all, in the hometown of a man known for performing miracles, I figured it must have been either by fate or divine intervention and there really was no reason to question either of those.

Of course, we had a couple of bottles of local wine to wash down all that incredible food, and for dessert my friend Antonio served us immaculate homemade coffee cake and espresso.

As at almost all Italian meals, the stories and the laughs flowed like the wine, and we ended the festivities by singing a few songs with Antonio and promising that we would visit again. Whether he would remember us or not.

It was after a glorious meal like that when I realized why Padre Pio wanted to be – needed to be – from Pietrelcina.

And something that I learned a little bit later about my friend Antonio sort of brings it all together: His last name, DiNunzio, is the maiden name of Padre Pio's mother, Maria Giuseppa DiNunzio Forgione. Go ahead, you can look it up.

I mean, Antonio couldn't be... nah.

He couldn't possibly be related to... no, that's crazy... to Padre Pio? Or could he?

Either way, if it's not a heavenly town, it sure is a magical one.

29

Their Pride Is Showing

Maiori, Provincia di Salerno, Campania (Amalfi Coast)

Chi dorme non piglia pesci. – *Traditional Italian proverb*

Literally: One who sleeps does not catch the fish.

English equivalent: The early bird catches the worm.

More info: The significant impact that the sea has on the lives of many Italians is highlighted in the phrase, as well as the fact that one of the most enduring professions in Italy's history is that of a fisherman. Another Italian proverb referencing the sea is the counterpart to the English "Easier said than done:" *Tra il dire e il fare c'è di mezzo il mare,* literally "Between saying and doing there is a sea in the middle."

The grilled fish – coming as it did, Italian-style with head and eyes quite intact – wasn't exactly what our friend envisioned when she ordered it at a seafood restaurant in the Amalfi Coast town of Maiori. The fish she was used to dining on back in the United States didn't eyeball her back from the plate.

So, she told the waiter that she was sorry, but she just couldn't eat it, and he cast her a look with eyes so sad and so woefully expressive that you would have thought someone killed his dog. Or his sea bass.

"Ah, but that is such a shame," he said in his best broken English. "This fish, this beautiful *branzino,* she was swimming happily in the sea this morning. Our local fishermen caught her and brought her here to our restaurant, and then just a few minutes ago, our chef prepared it wonderfully, with tender loving affection, only for you to-night, madam."

It was meant as the ultimate sales pitch, at least in his mind, high-lighting – all in one swoop – the freshness of the fish, the adroitness of the anglers who brought her in, and the culinary skills of the kitchen staff.

But sorry, our friend wasn't buying. Or eating. Head and eyeballs intact? No sale.

(And in case you're wondering, it's said that a fish cooked whole, head and all, is much more delicious and much more flavorful than its filleted counterpart, similar to the way chicken with the bone in and skin on tastes better and juicier than skinless, boneless chicken … my Dad sums it up simply: "The head keeps the flavor in.")

Well, on this night the waiter took away the *branzino* – a delicate white fish found in Europe's seas and salt lakes – again, ever so sadly. But only after first asking everyone else at the table if any of us would like this jewel of the sea. Believe me, I gladly would have stepped up and taken it, eyeballs and all, except that I already had my own equally lovely fish, which also had been swimming quite joyfully in the Mediterranean that very same morning. I didn't think I could chow down two of those babies in one sitting.

The point of that tale, however, is to illustrate just how proud Italians are of everything they do, especially if it has to do with serving food or creating something, such as wine or cheese or artwork. My wife and I have noticed this often as we've traveled the Old Country – in fact, Jan notices it more than I do.

At the *Azienda Agricola Nieddu Giovannino,* a farm in San Casciano, Tuscany, where they make fresh pecorino and other cheeses every day, the only thing whiter than the curd used to make the *formaggio* were the toothy, full-out smiles of the owners, who doubled as the cheese makers.

At the *Fattoria Pulcino,* a restaurant and winery in the country-side near Montepulciano, the patrons raved so much about the delicious homemade food, especially the risotto with porcini mushrooms and the pappardelle with ragù, that the owner went back into the kitchen to pull out the cook, *Signora Gabriella*, so that she could receive her due from the cheering and appreciative diners. Take a bow, *mamma* Gabriella! (Yes, she was really her mother!)

Up in the marble mountains of Carrara, just imagine the pride of the sculptors as they took a raw block of marble and carved something stunning out of it – reliving the words of Michelangelo who, upon receiving praise for one of his statues would say, "This wonderful statue was already in the stone; all I did was chisel away the extraneous to reveal it."

And later, on a tour of some marble quarries, the quarrymen were incredibly proud to show us even the equipment that they used – complete with diamond-studded chains – to "carve" the raw marble out of the mountain.

Italians, it seems – everyone from artisans and winemakers to farmers and even common folks – take incredible pride in what they do, in the wine they make, in the animals they raise, in the macaroni they roll out and then boil. And it shows, usually in a big, wide "aw shucks" grin.

Perhaps the ultimate was a cooking class we took in Tuscany on one of our group trips. Husband-and-wife duo Massimo Marzi and Cecilia Dei took us into the kitchen of Poggio al Chiuso, a bed-and-breakfast – known as an *agriturismo* in Italy – they run in the heart of the Chianti region. They showed us the finer points of a handful of regional dishes, including "drunken pork" – *maiale ubriaco* – so named because it is braised in red wine (local Chianti, if you must know), a typical Tuscan bread-and-tomato soup called *pappa al pomodoro*, and exquisitely delicate *tiramisu* for dessert.

Then, after demonstrating the preparation and cooking process, they escorted our group to *Osteria La Gramola*, a restaurant they own in the pretty little town of Tavarnelle Val di Pesa, where they served us a dinner of – what else? – drunken pork, bread-and-tomato soup and exquisitely delicate tiramisu.

Imagine being so proud of what you do that you not only share your secrets and insider tips with a bunch of American strangers, but then you prepare the meal all over for them again at your restaurant. And yes, of course, they were smiling each and every step of the way, . especially when our group gave them a standing ovation.

Now, that is something of which to be proud.

30

Living Life
"Alla Prossima Volta"

Milano, Provincia di Milano, Lombardia

Che ne so. – Italian expression
American equivelant: How in the heck should I know? *(rather than the more precise and formal "Non lo so" or "I don't know.")*
What it means: Used as a sarcastic response to someone asking something that you don't (or couldn't possibly) know. A gesture typically accompanies this phrase ... a shrug of the shoulders and wavering hands turned toward the sky as you shake your head "no."

I have long been an admirer of the lifestyle in our favorite Old Country which I believe helps them live longer and more stress-free than we do in America.

The Italians have a saying, for example, that they apply to numerous situations: *Alla prossima volta*. Often, they shorten it to *alla prossima* or even more simply, just *prossima*. It literally means "until next time" or "next time." Most often it is used to say goodbye or see you later. But it also seems to be a catch-all to be used in a context such as this: "What? You forgot to get the olive oil at the store? Ah, don't worry about it; you can get it next time."

To Italians, there's always a next time. Don't stress, don't worry, you can make it up. Next time.

Hey, you couldn't make it to the party today? *OK, alla prossima –* next time.

You didn't bring grandma her favorite cheesecake? Ok, don't forget next time. *Alla prossima.*

I was glad I was armed with the *alla prossima* knowledge on a group trip in 2013 to northern Italy. Milan was the starting point for an adventure that would take us to Lake Como, Verona and Venice. Our initial stop was at the historic Sforza Castle, built in the 15th century upon 14th-century fortifications; then we moved on to exploring the 400-year-old Ambrosiana Library. Founded in 1609 by Cardinal Federico Borromeo and named for Ambrose, the patron saint of Milan, the library also houses the Pinacoteca Ambrosiana, an incredible art gallery that contains works by Leonardo DaVinci, Raffaello, Caravaggio and Botticelli.

We had just walked under a version of DaVinci's famous "Last Supper" painted on a wall above a doorway about 1615 by Andrea Bianchi, a disciple of the great Leonardo. Better known as *"Il Vespino"* – which as far as I can figure through various translation websites basically means "The Vespino" – Bianchi was commissioned to do the copy because the master's original, completed in 1497, already was falling into disrepair.

(Interesting to note here, that both DaVinci's original "Last Supper" and Bianchi's version both are still going strong, a combined 900-plus years after they were created, and they reside in buildings in Milan that are about three blocks from each other, Da Vinci's being housed in the refectory of the Convent of *Santa Maria delle Grazie*).

From the room with Bianchi's "Last Supper," we walked into the historic library itself, and I felt as if I had stepped into a scene from a Dan Brown novel. The walls of the two-story room were lined with centuries-old books and manuscripts, treatises on religion, science, the humanities, the antiquities, medicine. It contains love letters between Lucrezia Borgia and Pietro Bembo – called "The prettiest love letters in the world" by Lord Byron – and was the second public library in Europe after the Bodleian Library in Oxford. It reminded me of Hobart and William Smith Colleges' Blackwell Room, in my small city of Geneva,

New York, but if you have ever been to *any* old-style library with rich, heavy mahogany shelves, lush carpeting and drapes, you have an idea of what that library looks like. Just picture larger, older and somewhat more ornate.

Several popes looked down upon us in paintings from the second floor, surely praying for our souls. However, the highlight for me was that the Ambrosiana Library contains a display of DaVinci writings and drawings called the *Codex Atlanticus*, a 12-volume set of sketches and musings from the genius himself. Or at least it did on that trip; my understanding is that it was a traveling exhibit that also was going to spend some time in Los Angeles and other locales.

Housed in more than a dozen glass display cases that wrapped around the library's main floor were some of DaVinci's notes, designs, drawings and thoughts on a wide range of subjects: weaponry, flight, mathematics, musical instruments, and the human body. There was a design for a giant crossbow, others for war armaments, water wheels, parachutes and underwater vessels.

And I mean, they were right there, separated from the public by only knee-level red velvet ropes like you might see in a movie theater. You could lean over the ropes and get your face so close to Leonardo's precious works that you could fog up the glass.

The boys back home just weren't going to believe this, so I had to take some photos, especially of the drawings of flying machines, pulleys, catapults, anatomy, even raindrops and water.

Throughout the museum there had been signs indicating that flash photography was not permitted. Photos, as far as I understood, were OK but no brilliant flashes that could disturb these delicate and priceless books and works of art.

The library had no such sign, at least that I could see, but I assumed the rules were the same – no flash. So, I made sure the flash was off on my camera – and yes, I'm talking a real 35mm camera here, kids, not a cellphone or an iPad – and I took about eight or ten shots, some so close and detailed that when I look at them I want to go build a flying machine myself.

After stepping back to soak up the history and the atmosphere one last time, I made my way toward the exit, passing a security guard to whom I nodded.

He looked a little like Woody Allen, an Italian Woody Allen, with arms folded across his chest, and I was caught off guard when he said, "No photos."

"Excuse me?" I offered.

"No photos," he repeated.

I said, in my best Italian, "I realize flash is prohibited, but I thought I could take photos in here without a flash."

Woody unfolded his arms, stuck out the index finger on his right hand and waved it from side to side, scolding me. I don't know exactly how this translates into Italian, but he basically said, "Tsk ... tsk ... tsk ... no photos," his head cocked a bit to the side and his eyebrows raised in one of those "Do we understand each other?" looks.

But no, I didn't understand. Plus, I already had taken the photos. He had watched me take them. I thought, "Why didn't you stop me after the first one? Plus, can't you see now that I am on my way out?" In my mind's eye, I envisioned us tussling over my Canon, with this pipsqueak Woody Allen look-alike attempting to wrestle it away from me and rip the film out like in those old movies.

Then I remembered, wait ... it was a digital camera. It didn't have film.

I didn't really know where we were supposed to go from here, but I did recall that Italian attitude thing, so I told Woody, "Listen, next time I come in here, sir, I will not take any photos. I promise. *Alla prossima volta*, no photos ..."

Woody nodded contentedly, refolded those arms across his chest and went back to guarding those precious artifacts from those scoundrel, photo-taking tourists.

So, just remember next time you're stuck in a little bit of a precarious situation, especially if you find yourself in a 400-year-old library in Milano about to throw down with a Woody Allen double, it might be worth playing the *alla prossima* card.

31

A Sicilian Adventure

Valguarnera Caropepe, Provincia di Enna, Sicilia

In bocca al lupo. – *Traditional Italian saying*

Literally: In the mouth of the wolf.

What it means: Good luck.

Background: Some say it harkens back to the story of Romulus and Remus, twins who were abandoned as infants, then discovered and suckled to health by a she-wolf; the boys went on to found the city of Rome. Others say it means "to aim into the wolf's mouth" to kill it, the wolf representing a difficulty that is being faced. When wishing that someone overcomes something even more serious, the saying is *"Crepi il lupo,"* literally, "Croak the wolf," like when we say, "You'll beat it" or "You'll kill it."

As we tooled along in the rental car – a shiny, dark blue Fiat Punto – on twisting, hilly highways and the smaller, regional roads of central Sicily, I could feel my wife's excitement in the seat next to me.

She was wearing her prettiest dress, had her hair done up just right, and I could only imagine the thoughts that were going through her head as she gazed out the window on our way to Valguarnera Caropepe.

If you haven't heard of Valguarnera Caropepe it's because it is not the most famous of Sicilian towns — those would be Palermo, Catania, Agrigento, and Taormina – but to Jan, it is perhaps the most important. It is where her maternal grandfather, Gregorio Miraglia, was born and where he lived until he was 9 years old when, in 1910, he left with his mother for America. It was a town few in Jan's family had even heard of; at least not until her Aunt Kay researched things and put together a family history a few years earlier. And it most certainly was one that no one from the family had ever visited.

That is until September 19, 2015 when we visited. As you may realize by now, I adore this kind of thing.

You already have read about our excursion to the Lazio region and the city of Frosinone in search of Jan's paternal grandfather, Pietro Mastracci. So, here we were – on the road again – on another family history expedition.

But first, a little more background, compliments of Aunt Kay:

Gregorio (or Gregory) Miraglia arrived at Ellis Island on March 18, 1910 with his mother, Gaetana DiGregorio, his sisters Lucia and Angelina, and a brother, Gaetano. He eventually would meet and marry Salvatrice (Sarah) Iacuzzo, who was born in Rochester, New York, but whose parents also were from Sicily. Gregory and Sarah would have eight children, including Jan's Mom, Josephine – or Josie, for short.

I shorten it even further to Jo and must admit that she has been a godsend to me since my own Mom went to that big library in the sky.

I won't tell you how old she is, but I will tell you she was born the same year as my Dad, in fact, the same year that the Empire State Building was completed, the classic films "Dracula" and "Frankenstein" were released and the "Star-Spangled Banner" was officially adopted as America's national anthem.

If you figure the year out, we'll have a toast with her favorite wine, Giacobazzi Lambrusco.

With Jo, that whole age thing is really to say that no matter what her birth certificate might state, her zest for life is unmatched. Most 25-year-olds I know couldn't keep up with her in a grocery store. Need a load of laundry done? No problem dropping it off at her place, because, after all, as she says, "The machine does all the work."

The neat little white house in Lyons, New York, where she and her husband John live is always filled with laughter, love and a little bit of needling. And did I mention she's a magician with a pasta maker, especially rolling out dough for her signature ravioli? Just make sure that the ricotta cheese isn't too "loose" (you'll have to ask her if you need to know what that means or if you want a one-on-one lesson in making that dough durable yet thin).

So, as a tribute to my mother-in-law – and with a goal of shooting lots of photographs to bring back to show her where her father grew up – I planned this little day trip to Valguarnera Caropepe with her daughter.

We were on a group trip exploring the fascinating island of sunny Sicily that fall. Three nights were going to be spent in Agrigento on the southern coast, famous for its incredibly well-preserved Greek temples. Before we left the States, though, I noticed on a map that while we were in Agrigento we would be only about an hour's drive from Valguarnera Caropepe. So, we made plans to break off the tour for a day, rent that Fiat and go in search of Jan's heritage.

There are no connections between Jan's Miraglia family and Valguarnera Caropepe today, at least not that anyone knows of, but again before we left, I went on whitepages.com and found the phone numbers of six Miraglia families in Valguarnera. I was going to call all six myself, but when I explained the situation to Andrea, our tour guide from Bologna, he offered to make the calls for us. As much as I enjoy speaking Italian and basically can get by, I figured we'd be much better off with a native working the phone, especially since these calls would be coming from way, way, *way* out of the blue.

Andrea – a man's name that means Andrew in Italian, by the way – called all six families and explained Jan's situation. He asked all the Miraglias if they had a Gregorio in the family line, especially one who may have emigrated off to America as a youngster in 1910. Unfortunately, all said no … or that they did not know.

Except for 85-year-old Francesco Miraglia who said that even though there was no one named Gregorio Miraglia in his family, he knew a woman who he thought had an uncle Gregorio Miraglia. Because she was married, her name did not show up on my internet search for

Via Della Stazione in Valguarnera Caropepe, home of the Profeta family.

Miraglia. So, Francesco told us he was going to call Miranda Profeta to explain the situation and then would call us back.

Andrea, a beautiful and helpful person in his own right whose charge is to make the trips of his American customers as memorable as possible, was genuinely as excited as we were on making this "connection."

Within 10 minutes, his cellphone rang. It was Miranda Profeta herself! She extended an invitation for Jan and me to stop at her home in downtown Valguarnera. I thought I detected a tear of joy in Andrea's eye ... to say nothing of the tears that rolled down Jan's cheeks. "There you go, all set up for you," Andrea told us. *"In bocca al lupo."*

The next day, after picking up the Fiat in bustling downtown Agrigento, we were off on our magnificent adventure, which began with the lovely drive itself through central Sicily, a part of the island that most tourists do not experience. Valguarnera is in the Province of Enna, which is the only one of Sicily's nine provinces that is completely landlocked; there are 1,000 miles of coastline on Sicily, but none touch this inland province. The hilltop city of Enna, itself, is the capital of the region and often referred to as "The Navel of Sicily."

The land surrounding Valguarnera is agricultural – something that made Jan smile because she remembered her grandfather Greg as a farmer growing up in Lyons. That part of Sicily is noted primarily for rolling hills of wheat, but almonds, walnuts and of course, olives and grapes also are grown in abundance.

The town of Valguarnera Caropepe is unique to me because it is one of the only ones I know of in all of Italy that is named after a person, Francesco Valguarnera, who founded it in 1628. Caropepe derives from the Sicilian dialect word *Carrapipi*, which is the name of the hill upon which the town is built.

As we pulled into Gregorio Miraglia's hometown and began our search for Via Della Stazione where the Profeta family lived – stopping first to buy flowers to bring them – I could sense Jan's eagerness and knew her heart was racing. Me, I was just thrilled about experiencing another Italian exploration; this country has never failed to deliver.

We surmised that Miranda Profeta's uncle and Jan's grandfather were not the same man, but with the Italian tradition of naming children after others in the family, we had a strong sense that they were somehow related, one possibly the namesake of the other.

We found the Profetas' home relatively easily – nothing short of a miraculous feat in the small towns of Italy, if you have ever tried to do so – and were greeted warmly by Miranda's husband Liberio who was waiting for us out on the street. When we went inside, the welcoming party included Miranda's sister, who had spent time in Rochester, of all places, and Francesco Miraglia, who had made the connection for us (and sadly, has since passed away), along with Francesco's daughter Lara Miraglia.

Miranda had espresso ready for us along with a stack of family photographs on the dining room table. Our conversation – all in Italian – centered around trying to connect the dots between Jan and Miranda. Unfortunately, however, we were unable to. She showed us photos of her uncle Gregorio along with other family members, and Jan, through me as interpreter, told stories of what she remembered of her grandpa Gregorio.

Though we couldn't make the association right then and there at the table, my feeling is that if we go back another generation from Jan's grandfather, we will strike gold. We all promised we would continue the genealogical research on both ends.

In the meantime, we said: "*Se non siamo cugini, almeno siamo nuovi amici. Facciamo un brindisi a quello!*' If we are not cousins, at least we are new friends; let's have a toast to that!

We had a joyful and heart-felt toast, and then Lara took Jan and me on a tour of Valguarnera Caropepe, a centuries-old town that thrived in the late 18th and early 19th century because of a booming sulfur mining industry in the area. Lara showed us some of its nine churches – incredible, I thought, for a town of less than 8,000 people – including its largest, San Giuseppe. She showed us the main shopping area, the municipal building, and the bridal shop where she worked. She also took us to the highest point, where the water tower stood, that offered stunning views of the surrounding valley and distant hills.

A highlight of our *giro* – or tour – was a stop in a local cafe that was run by another Miraglia family, Salvatore and his son Calogero. We took pictures of the three Miraglias – Jan, Lara and Calogero – unsure but hopeful that they might be three *cugini* – or cousins.

When our tour was finished, we drove back to the Profetas' home where Miranda had prepared a lovely *pranzo* (lunch) for us. It included spaghetti with homemade *pomodoro* sauce, two types of eggplant dishes, one fried and one baked, and fresh, crispy salad. Everything on the table was either home grown on their farm just outside of town, or homemade, including the spaghetti. We washed it down with Liberio's homemade wine and toasted at the conclusion with homemade *limoncello*. We capped the *pranzo* with more espresso and some typical Sicilian pastries that Jan and I bought at a little bakery that Lara took us to.

The Profetas' daughter Sonia and her husband joined us after lunch, and the stories whirling around the table included those about my own Italian background and where my father and relatives had come from. It truly was a memorable day, and even though we were unable to make the family connection that we had been in search of, at the very least a strong bond was formed, and we vowed to stay in touch, which we have. Liberio also told us that we were no longer allowed to stay in any hotels in Sicily; any time we visit in the future, we must stay with them, he said, in Jan's grandfather's hometown.

We closed by saying: *"Anche se siamo solamente amici a questo punto, ci sentiamo più come cugini. Quindi, siamo amici-cugini!"* Even though we are only friends at this point, we feel more like cousins – so, we are "friend-cousins!"

We laughed at the new term we had coined, and then Jan and I parted. All of us had tears in our eyes.

Have I mentioned that Italy never fails to deliver?

32

Chasing History -
And A Good Cocktail

Venezia, Provincia di Venezia, Veneto:

"Ma che cosa posso raccontare a questa ragazza, ora, in questa fredda mattina ventosa al Gritti Palace Hotel?"
"Che cosa vorresti sapere, Figlia?" le chiese.
"Tutto quanto."
"Va bene," disse il colonnello. "Incominciamo."
— Ernest Hemingway, "Across the River and into the Trees"

"But what can I tell this girl, now, on this cold, windy morning at the Gritti Palace Hotel?"
"What would you like to know, Daughter?" he asked.
"Everything."
"All right," said the colonel. "Let us begin."

Venezia è come mangiare un'intera scatola di cioccolata al liquore in una sola volta. – Truman Capote
Literally: Venice is like eating an entire box of chocolate liqueurs at once.
What it means: Venice is a city that arouses all the senses, and the more you dig into it, the more you are addicted to it.

I enjoy chasing history. I also enjoy a good cocktail every now and again. When I can combine the two, I am in heaven.

If I told you Ernest Hemingway wrote those sentences, would you believe me?

My daughter Kristine. We had a front-row seat as bartender, Gabriele, whipped up a batch of Bellinis.

How about if I told you that I wrote them after hanging out in a joint that Hemingway used to frequent in Venice – aka "The Queen of the Adriatic" and "The City of Canals" – then would you believe me?

That's the effect throwing back a cocktail – OK, two cocktails, if you must know – had on me during an afternoon with my daughter Kristine in *bella Venezia* at Harry's Bar, a stone's throw from St. Mark's square and the Grand Canal and a longtime Bucket List objective of mine.

There are other Harry's Bars around the world, but the original one is in Venice, founded in 1931 by Giuseppe Cipriani and run today by his son Arrigo and his grandson Giuseppe. It is one of the world's iconic bars, at least in my rankings. Its staff is credited with inventing both a famous cocktail (the Bellini) and a famous dish (Carpaccio), both of which were named after famous painters. Try finding that doubleheader at any other establishment on the planet. Also, in true historic, Italian, connect-the-dots fashion, Vittore Carpaccio studied painting under Gentile Bellini, sometime in the late 1400s.

Harry's is not particularly lavish, other than the stunning, shiny, wood-trimmed bar, but it oozes style and class, the way a young Sinatra did in those black-and-white photo days. The barmen wear sharp, crisp, white jackets and pressed dress shirts along with black bow ties. Everything is neat and clean, and it's said that – long before it was a phrase associated with Las Vegas – whatever happens at Harry's, stays at Harry's.

Hemingway was indeed a fixture during the long winter of 1949-50 and beyond. Scenes in his 1950 novel "Across the River and Into the Trees" – which is quoted at the beginning of this chapter – are set at Harry's, and you can still sit at the corner table that the great American novelist known as Papa preferred while sipping his gin martinis and holding court.

The great author is said to have had a complex love affair with Venice, the city of the Rialto Bridge, the Bridge of Sighs and amazing seafood such as *sarde in saor* (sweet-and-sour sardines with onions) and *scampi alla veneziana* (fresh boiled shrimp in olive oil and lemon juice). He was wounded while serving for the American Red Cross near Venice in World War I and later scorned the man who would drag Italy into World War II, Benito Mussolini, calling him "the biggest bluff in Europe" in a 1923 newspaper article. Mussolini countered by banning Hemingway's "A Farewell to Arms," a best-seller set during the Italian campaign in World War I that many consider among his best works.

Hemingway stayed away from Italy for decades but by the late 1940s, her beguiling allure was just too much, and he returned, setting up shop in Venice and becoming a fixture at Harry's.

In typical Italian fashion, where everything seems to have a story, there is, of course, a good one about how Harry's got its name.

Before founding Harry's, Giuseppe Cipriani was tending bar at a place called Hotel Europa. One of the regulars was Harry Pickering, a young American who came not only from Boston but from money.

When Pickering stopped coming in, Cipriani learned that, because of his drinking habits, his family had cut him off financially, and he had run out of money. The good-hearted Giuseppe loaned him 10,000 *lire*, a princely-sounding sum that amounted to about $500 at the time, though that probably was indeed a princely total back then.

A couple of years later, after rebounding, Pickering sauntered into the hotel bar, ordered a drink and handed over 50,000 *lire* to Cipriani, telling him, according to the Cipriani website: "Mr. Cipriani, thank you. Here's the money. And to show you my appreciation, here's 40,000 more, enough to open a bar. We will call it Harry's Bar."

How about raising a glass to that story?

Harry's was named a national landmark by the Italian government in 2001, and when Giuseppe had a son a year after the bar opened, he named him Arrigo – Harry, in Italian.

Truman Capote used to hang there. So did Orson Welles, Jimmy Stewart, Alfred Hitchcock, Peggy Guggenheim and Aristotle Onassis. Among folks who happen to still be breathing, Woody Allen, Helen Hunt and Nicole Kidman have been known to pull up a bar stool. I asked our barman, Gabriele, who he would say was the most famous person to visit recently, and he answered American actor George Clooney, during his wedding celebration.

I couldn't verify that on the internet, although Clooney did reportedly host a dinner for friends and relatives at Hotel Cipriani, on the Venetian island of Giudecca, just to the south of St. Mark's. Because that exclusive hotel also was founded by our friend Giuseppe Sr., I figure it's close enough, so I will give Gabriele a pass.

That's the historical part.

Now, for that drink: My daughter, I'm happy to say, playing along with her Dad's Bucket List Adventure, ordered up a Bellini (sparkling Prosecco wine, famous in the Veneto region, and white peach purée), to which Gabriele, who was from Udine in the nearby Friuli-Venezia Giulia region, smiled and said, "Ah, that is our classic; I am very happy to make that just for you." I went with another classic Italian cocktail, a Negroni (gin, vermouth and Campari).

There are only six stools at the small bar, and we occupied two of them – ideal front-row seats to chat with Gabriele (about his 3-month-old daughter, Italian soccer, and then-American President Barack Obama) and watch him cruise through the preparation of those two drinks like the seasoned mixologist he is.

The cocktails were exquisite ... and crazy expensive, just as I had expected. The Bellini was 18 Euros (about $20), and the Negroni was only a couple of Euros less. It's interesting because I had looked up some reviews of Harry's on TripAdvisor.com before we visited, and the words "overpriced," "not worth the money" and "there are cheaper places to drink" came up often.

I'm no high roller by a long shot, but I look at it this way: It is what it is. Just as bad reviews of a film that I really want to see won't stop me from going to see it, negative online reviews of Harry's Bar weren't going to stop me from my appointed rounds. Besides, you don't go to Harry's to save a Euro or two. You go to soak up all that atmosphere ... and to drink with those famous ghosts.

Speaking of ghosts, Gabriele must have thought he was serving one because the next time he whipped up a couple of Bellinis at the request of one of his waiters, he was told by that waiter that he had only asked for one, not two. With an extra, brand-new, freshly-made Bellini sitting there in all its peach lusciousness just waiting to be sipped, Gabriele easily could have just poured it down the sink. Instead, he looked at my daughter and asked her if she would like another Bellini ... on the house!

So there, all you Trip Advisor negative reviewers. With a little fortuitousness and perhaps because we were channeling the ghost of Hemingway, we had our own little Harry's Happy Hour two-for-one that day. How's that for a special memory?

Oh, there's one other thing about Harry's Bar, though: Gentlemen don't wear shorts there after 6 p.m.

So, shorts-wearing American tourist that I was, as the clock ticked toward 6, my daughter and I had to bid *arrivederci* to Gabriele. As reputation has it, if I had been able to pop into Harry's again the next day, and if Gabriele was working, he would have said: "Good day, sir. Can I get you your regular?"

I came across a 2001 article in the British newspaper The Guardian about Harry's in which the head barman at the time, a Claudio Ponzio, was asked how Harry's had changed over the years.

"In the 32 years I've worked in Harry's Bar I don't believe it has changed at all, we have simply grown old together. That is the secret of its unique success."

A throwback that never changed ... a speakeasy in the good sense, discreet, not much in the way of signage, its reputation proliferated mainly by word of mouth ... barkeeps who are good listeners but can spin a tale as well.

Another thing that makes it special: the personal touch. I wrote an account for the newspaper of Kristine's and my day at Harry's and somehow Arrigo Cipriani saw it on the internet. A few days later, he sent me an email saying, in part, "I'm sorry I missed you and your daughter that day. I probably was there later because I still regularly go to Harry's, but I usually get there after 6 p.m. Please let me know the next time you are in Harry's because I would like to meet you."

So, I've got that going for me, which is nice.

Anyway, after a special day with my daughter and having indulged two of my passions – history and adult beverages – I will close the way Hemingway might have ... of course, with all due respect to the man known as Papa.

We pulled open the door of Harry's Bar, entered, and stepped back in time. The cocktails were familiar, fabulous. The ambiance was even better, marvelous really.

Life is good. Or as they say in Italian, la vita è bella.

33

A Real-life Movie Set

Palazzo Adriano, Provincia di Palermo, Sicilia

ALFREDO: Fino a quando ci stai tutti i giorni, ti senti al centro del mondo. Ti sembra che non cambia mai niente. Poi parti, un anno, due, e quando torni é cambiato tutto. Si rompe il filo. Non trovi che volevi trovare. Le tue cose non ci sono più. Bisogna andare via per molto tempo, per moltissimi anni, per ritrovare al ritorno la tua gente, la terra dove sei nato. Ma ora no, non é possibile. Ora tu sei più cieco di me.

SALVATORE (TOTÒ): Questa chi l'ha detta? Gary Cooper, James Stewart, Henry Fonda?

ALFREDO: No, Totò. Non l'ha detto proprio nessuno. Questo lo dico io. La vita non é come l'hai visto al cinematografo. La vita é più difficile.

– From the movie "Nuovo Cinema Paradiso"

ALFREDO: Living here day by day, you think it's the center of the world. You believe nothing will ever change. Then you leave: a year, two years. When you come back, everything's changed. The thread's broken. What you came to find isn't there. What was yours is gone. You must go away for a long time … many years … before you can come back and find your people, the land where you were born. But now, no, it's not possible. Right now, you're blinder than I am.

SALVATORE (TOTÒ): Who said that? Gary Cooper, James Stewart, Henry Fonda?

ALFREDO: No, Totò. Nobody said it. This time it's all me. Life isn't like in the movies. Life … is much harder.

The 55-passenger coach wound its way up the twisting mountain road, not so much rolling, as buses are more normally known to travel, but more like inching along. Even though the huge vehicle was slick and tight, with a motor manufactured by Mercedes Benz, you could almost hear it groan. Gianni, our bus driver, worked the gears, the brakes, and the steering wheel like an orchestra maestro, negotiating the hairpin turns and the narrow, winding road, and that's to say nothing of the drama that ensued whenever the coach would be met by traffic coming in the opposite direction. This road – SS188, if you're scoring at home – was not built for anything other than a couple of donkeys hauling carts. But up the mountain we climbed, up, up ... up some more; seemingly, always up.

I had asked Gianni the night before what he thought about this particular portion of our two-week tour of Sicily in 2015, and he told me it would be a *"pesante"* – or a "heavy" – workday for him. It was an Italian bus driver's way to say that there would be no vino that evening; he needed a good night's sleep.

We were in the mountains in the northwest portion of the island, halfway between Palermo to the north and Agrigento to the south, on our way to the tiny village of Palazzo Adriano.

If you've never heard of it, you're not alone. Palazzo Adriano with its 2,000 or so residents does not show up on most itineraries of Sicily. Our tour guide Andrea Blasi estimated that one in a thousand tour buses makes the 2,300-foot, harrowing climb up Monte delle Rose to visit the mountaintop village that was an Albanian settlement when it was founded around the year 1000.

So that made our group 1-in-1,000, I guess. Here's the deal, though, when you dream up these group-trip itineraries – as I have for more than 10 years now – you can go to places that you want to go to and lug everyone else along for the ride. A good friend of mine, Mike Rusinko, was on this trip with his wife Carol, and a few days earlier – while we relaxed with a glass of wine on the patio of our adjoining hotel rooms in San Leone, near Agrigento and a stone's throw across the Mediterranean from Tunisia and Africa – he said, "I get this ... I finally get this. We are on Mike Cutillo's Fantasy Tour. You dream up these amazing trips, and then you drag 50 or so friends along with you. I get it."

He had figured me out.

But whatever. I had dreamed of seeing Palazzo Adriano ever since I learned that most of the scenes in one of my favorite movies of all-time, "Nuovo Cinema Paradiso," were filmed there. And, in fact, Andrea, an experienced guide from Bologna, way up north on the mainland, had put in a bid with his travel agency to be the guide for this particular trip because he had been to Sicily over 20 times but had never been to Palazzo Adriano, which he also had always wanted to see; Gianni, our bus driver and a native of Sicily from the city of *Siracusa*, also had never been to Palazzo Adriano.

If you don't know the movie – which won an Academy Award and a Golden Globe for Best Foreign Film in 1989 – I won't give away the plot. But I will tell you that in addition to being a movie about going to the movies in post-World War II Sicily, it also is a touching love story. In fact, it's a couple of love stories, the main one being a platonic one between a grown man, Alfredo, the projectionist at the local movie theater, and Salvatore, nicknamed Totò, a precocious young boy who, in the opening scene of the movie, is scolded for nodding off during Mass while he served as an altar boy. Alfredo becomes the father figure that Totò lost when his own father was killed in the war.

In addition to beautiful cinematography and a great script, it has a hauntingly sweet, award-winning score by Ennio Morricone, the legendary composer who also wrote the score for, among many other films, "The Good, the Bad and the Ugly."

I've seen "Cinema Paradiso" described as an example of "nostalgic postmodernism," mixing sentimentality with comedy and nostalgia with pragmatism. I'm not sure I'm smart enough to know what all that means. I can tell you that it is, however, a coming-of-age film that uses flashbacks to reflect upon youth that morphs into adulthood. It was a critical and box-office success and almost instantly gained the status of a classic when it was released worldwide in 1990; in a 2017 ranking of "The

A shot of the house in Palazzo Adriano on which Alfredo projected a movie outdoors for the villagers.

100 Best Films of World Cinema" by Empire Magazine, it was ranked No. 27 all-time. Renowned film critic Roger Ebert, in a March 1990 review of the film for the *Chicago Sun-Times*, wrote, "Anyone who loves movies is likely to love 'Cinema Paradiso.' ... Romances are launched in the darkness of the theater, friendships are sealed, wine is drunk, cigarettes smoked, babies nursed, feet stomped, victories cheered, sissies whistled at, and god only knows how this crowd would react if they were ever permitted to see a kiss." That's a reference to one of the key recurring themes of the film: the local priest who, in addition to being annoyed by Totò, pre-screens all the films that are shown at the theater and has Alfredo clip out scurrilous love scenes; love scenes, by the way, that are incredibly tame by today's standards.

In short, though, if you haven't seen "Nuovo Cinema Paradiso," you should buy the DVD or get it on Netflix or stream it or something like that.

It is set in the fictitious town of Giancaldo, which I did not know was fictitious until I tried to look it up and found out it didn't exist.

I learned Giancaldo was based on another Sicilian town near Palermo called Bagheria, the hometown of the film's director, Giuseppe Tornatore. He selected Palazzo Adriano for much of the filming because even in 1988 – high atop that mountain – it had been preserved in time and still retained the feel of a post-WWII village that was called for in the script. It was so isolated, we were told, that many of the actors and crew were helicoptered in and stayed for weeks at a time while the filming was going on. Our bus driver Gianni could vouch for how isolated it was.

Not everyone in our group of 50 had seen the film, but I figured even those who hadn't would at the very least get to experience what a real off-the-beaten-path Sicilian mountaintop village looked and felt like with its main piazza, Piazza Umberto I, its narrow dusty streets and its weathered, life-long residents. For those of us who did know the film, when Gianni finally pulled that huge coach into town, it was like pulling onto a real-life movie set.

Everything was exactly as it was in the film, except for the movie theater itself. The Paradiso "cinema" was built specifically for the film and was not an actual part of the town. The Paradiso actually burns down in the movie, is rebuilt into the new – or "*nuovo*" – Paradiso and then is demolished toward the end when the fad of going to the movie house had died out.

So, no movie house. But there was the clock tower of Santa Maria del Lume ... and the town square with the Baroque-style water fountain that was built in 1608 in the center ... and the house on which Alfredo projects a film outdoors to the villagers' delight ... and another church, Chiesa Maria SS Assunta, in front of which local women spread tomatoes on wooden boards to dry into paste in the sun in a scene from the film. Gianni, who of course knew the film very well as most Italians do, was so enthralled that he pulled his huge Mercedes Benz tourist coach right up into the iconic main *piazza* and took pictures of it next to the water fountain; in a modern-day twist, he quickly and proudly posted those photos on Facebook. Just a man and his 50-passenger coach.

Andrea learned that the village hall contained a mini museum that featured photo stills from the film, along with a number of props, including a bicycle that Alfredo rode, and even a miniature model of what was supposed to be Giancaldo in the movie, complete with the movie theater. Thanks to Andrea calling ahead, our group was treated to a fascinating lecture on the making of the film from a village official, all in Italian and translated by Andrea. Among other things that we learned in the talk was that the actor Salvatore Cascio, who played the young Totò, was a boy who not only was from Palazzo Adriano, but whose nickname was really Totò, as many Salvatores, especially in Sicily, are nicknamed. You can't make this stuff up.

After the lecture, our group of 50 Americans descended upon the village that, remember, hosts very few tour buses. Our folks made quick friends with the villagers – Carmen Fratto, who looks like he could fit right in with the card-playing local men – received a dinner invite as did a couple of others. We helped the Palazzo Adriano economy by buying some of the few souvenirs that were available and took turns drinking the fresh, cool mountain spring water that ran through the piazza's iconic fountain, just like the folks did in the movie.

As I mentioned, this was something of a selfish stop on our Sicilian adventure – which also included more traditional venues such as Taormina and Palermo, Marsala and Agrigento – but judging by the contended smiles on the faces of those who knew the movie, and even from those who didn't, it was a magical success.

And was quite worth Gianni's "*pesante*" drive.

34

A Meeting With The 'Butcher of Panzano'

Panzano in Chianti, Provincia di Firenze, Toscana

Avere il prosciutto sugli occhi. – *Old Italian saying*

Literally: To have ham over your eyes.

What it means: If your eyes are covered by ham, you can't see anything, or you must pretend. Similarly, Americans say, "Burying your head in the sand like an ostrich."

Chi non carneggia non festeggia. – *Old Italian saying*

Literally: He who doesn't eat meat, doesn't celebrate.

L'amore vive non solo di sentimento ma di bistecche.
– *Carlo Dossi, Italian writer, politician, diplomat*

Literally: Love lives not just by sentiment but by steaks.

To beef or not to beef!?

To Dario Cecchini, the famous Tuscan butcher/poet/comedian/ philosopher, that is both a question and a declaration. And if you used it as a query and asked him, chances are he would look at you with his expressive steel-blue eyes, raise his meat cleaver that looks like it could slice through a Buick and exclaim, "*Sì!!*"

Or he might even quote Dante's famous "Inferno." Or a Rolling Stones song.

Dario Cecchini laughs with our group from behind the counter at his famous Antica Macelleria Cecchini in downtown Panzano.

Or he may just unfurl that famous broad smile that he has flashed on food and travel shows from Anthony Bourdain to Rick Steves, go back behind the counter in his world-renowned butcher shop, *Antica Macelleria Cecchini* – perhaps THE most famous and most iconic *macelleria* in all of Italy – turn up the volume on whatever rock song he happens to have going (it was Guns N' Roses' "Welcome to the Jungle" the day we were there) and get back to carving up the biggest slab of beef you've ever laid eyes upon.

America has its "celebrity chefs," people such as Bobby Flay and Gordon Ramsay, Giada De Laurentiis and Rachael Ray. Dario Cecchini – pronounced chay-KEE-nee – is Italy's answer. To many he is quite simply the most famous butcher in the world, although calling him a butcher does not seem to do justice to the versatile "Molto Dario." It's like saying a Lamborghini is just a car.

We had a chance to meet him on a 2017 group trip to Tuscany, and even with so many highlights in that most famous region of Italy – from the spectacular Duomo in Florence to Pisa's Leaning Tower to the curvy, cypress tree-lined roads of Chianti – visiting with him was the most unforgettable experience and the clear highlight for a food fan like me. Honestly, when I asked my friend and tour guide Rossana Anselmi if she could arrange for our large group of travelers to meet Cecchini, I never thought she would be able to pull it off. Somehow or other, however, she and her husband, Riccardo Carusi, both natives of Tuscany – Riccardo, in fact, is from the same small Tuscan village that produced Andrea Bocelli – used their home region connections to nail it down.

Flamboyantly Italian in his red, white and green-striped shirt, snow-white apron, bright red pants and red Crocs, Cecchini is like a boisterous, one-man Broadway show. He speaks English well enough – thanks primarily to his wife Kim, who is from California – but he prefers to philosophize in his native Italian, even if you don't understand, and especially when he is reciting poetry or speaking about his love for the animals that end up turning into your dinner.

Dario was born in 1955 in Panzano, a small town of about 1,000 residents – it isn't even a village but is called a *frazione* in Italian – where he is the eighth generation of his family to work slicing, dicing and chopping meat. Think about that for a second: The EIGHTH generation – is that quintessentially Italian or what? Panzano itself dates to the ancient Etruscans, who I'm thinking must have had a Cecchini butchering their meat for them.

Dario, though, did not initially plan on following in his family's cleaver-wielding lineage. Because of his empathy and reverence for critters he most assuredly was not going to become an eighth-generation butcher in the family but rather, quite the opposite. He was attending a veterinary school in Pisa in 1976, learning how to care for animals not plate them when he received word that his father was terminally ill. His mother already having died, he returned to his hometown of Panzano to care for his sister and grandmother. He also took over the family butcher shop, despite his fondness for animals, and eventually came to the realization that a butcher's path was not "detached from animals but beside them."

His own path to fame commenced in the early 2000s during the infamous Mad Cow Disease period. Called *mucca pazza* in Italian – literally "crazy cow" – the wide-ranging scourge had many people going beef-less. When the Italian government outlawed *bistecca alla fiorentina,* Tuscany's famous T-bone steak, because of that health scare, Cecchini organized and staged a dramatic mock funeral for the iconic cut of beef on March 31, 2001. His histrionics were picked up by a number of major news organizations around the globe. A plaque commemorating the ersatz somber day still hangs on the exterior wall at *Antica Macelleria Cecchini* in Panzano.

Newspaper and magazine articles followed, along with spots on numerous travel shows, including Bourdain's "No Reservations" and Kathy McCabe's "Dream of Italy," among others. His fame exploded. It is said that Dario's client list includes Prince Charles and Sting. In March of 2019, Netflix's documentary series "Chef's Table" featured Cecchini.

There are articles galore on the master *macellaio* so I won't get into additional details here. Suffice to say, however, if you ever find yourself near his hometown – whether by design or because you were chasing one of the region's infamous wild boars and lost track of where you were – do yourself a favor and look him up. You will be more than happy that you did. He will be, too.

In fact, the drive to Panzano is part of the package and one you'll undoubtedly remember as well. The *frazione* is on the Via Chiantigiana, which next to the Appian Way, may be Italy's most recognized and celebrated roadway. It is a picturesque, 45-mile artery that winds from Florence to Siena right through the middle of the sublimely scenic Chianti Classico wine zone.

When we arrived in Panzano – still incredulous that Rossana and Riccardo had managed to make this happen – we were met at *Antica Macelleria Cecchini* by Dario himself. He greeted us with outstretched arms and his signature *"Benvenuti ai tutti"* – "Welcome everyone." Rossana told us later that he had put off a last-minute trip to Bulgaria that day so that he could entertain this large group of Americans.

And entertain us he did. After the requisite photo ops with the star of the show, we enjoyed a few glasses of lovely Chianti wine, served to us by some of his employees in the street outside the shop (no "open container" law in Italy, thankfully!) along with wild boar salami that he had made, crostini with luscious extra-virgin Tuscan olive oil and a little history of that butcher shop and the Cecchini eight generations. While we were mingling and munching, Dario went behind the glass case of the small shop and began to do what he does best – have at that meat. A large man with what seem like bear paws for hands, he whipped our group into a frenzy that was accentuated by the loud rock music and the sound of his cleaver slamming through the thick slabs of beef and onto the cutting surface. Because only a handful of people at a time could fit in the small *macelleria*, we took turns wandering in to observe the master craftsman at work. One of Cecchini's charges is to protect and promote local butchers everywhere from the rise of supermarket chains, which are popping up even all over Italy these days, and he explained to our group that he believed traditional butchering was an artform that involved a healthy dose of appreciation and respect for the *mucca*. He also noted that all parts of the animal could be used if they were butchered and cooked properly. It was a lesson in *"carne"* – or meat – that captured everyone's attention, especially as the glasses of Chianti continued to go down.

In addition to restaurants around the world – a number that is growing along with his fame and includes the Caribbean – Cecchini also owns three eateries right in his little hometown of Panzano: *Officina delle Bistecca*, which is attached to his shop; *SoloCiccia*, which is just across the street; and *Dario Doc*.

After the show and *carne* lesson in *Antica Macelleria Cecchini*, our group was escorted to *Officina delle Bistecca* for an incredible *pranzo* – or lunch – that was served on long communal tables outdoors, under that renowned Tuscan sun with cloudless, bright blue skies. It was a five-course meal and all five courses included beef. Allow me to put that another way: It was a five-beef meal. It began with beef tartare and seared rump carpaccio. Next up was a bone-in ribeye, which was followed by a

Cecchini creation, a Panzanese-style steak – cut from one of those tough parts of the animal, the butt, grilled over red-hot coals and finished with just a few Tuscan spices and a drizzle of olive oil; if you think it was difficult to chew, think again, because it melted in your mouth. After all that, those of us who could still fit more beef into our stomachs were served the region's most famous dish, the fortunately no-longer-outlawed *bistecca alla fiorentina*, the three-finger-thick, rare-in-the-middle, seared-on-the-outside, T-bone steak that Dario had been butchering in his *macelleria* earlier. If you're scoring at home, that's right: Five courses … all meat. All butchered and prepared by Dario and his crew and each served up with an increasingly growing chorus of "ooohs and aaahs" from the diners.

There were sides of vegetables and potatoes – like we needed them, right? – and many more bottles of Chianti, which we did need to wash down all that beef.

It was loud and noisy, boisterous and happy, just as Dario likes a meal to be enjoyed. And every so often, while we were dining, the great showman/butcher himself would parade through our gathering, tooting a traditional Italian trumpet, stopping to pose for kisses, hugs and photos and exclaiming, always with a flourish, that namesake phrase: *To beef or not to beef!?!*

35

An 'Italian Palate'
Or When A Book Is More
Than A Book

Tavarnelle Val di Pesa, Provincia di Firenze, Toscana

La coincidenza ci farà incontrare e chiamalo destino quel percorso natura-
le che due puntini dentro l'universo raggiungono la strada che li illumina
d'immenso... – From "Arrivi Tu," a song by Daniele Coro and Federica Fratoni

Translation: Coincidence will make us meet and call it destiny, the natural path of two dots inside the universe will reach the road that illuminates them of immensity...

Le coincidenze sono il modo di Dio per rendersi anonimo. — Albert Einstein
Translation: Coincidences are God's way of making himself anonymous.

Le coincidenze, a volte, sono i segnali misteriosi della vita, ai quali bisogna
credere. – Romano Battaglia, Italian journalist and writer

Translation: Coincidences, at times, are the mysterious signs of life
that we have to believe in.

A few years ago, our friends Paul and Lisa Barrett gifted Jan and
me a coffee table book for our anniversary titled "An Italian Palate."

It was created – and hand-signed – by two folks they know from
their native Mississippi: writer and restauranteur Robert St. John and

watercolor artist extraordinaire Wyatt Waters. Writer and painter had spent nearly three months traveling throughout Italy, from Sicily in the south to Lake Como in the north, in search of traditional recipes (for Robert to write about) and beautiful scenes (for Wyatt to paint). "An Italian Palate" is a cookbook, a travelogue, a history book, and a collection of gorgeous photos and watercolors all wrapped into one hard-cover package.

Their sojourn also became as much, if not more, about the people they met along the way – the cooks and chefs; the restaurant, B&B and bar owners; even just the everyday folks in *piazze* all over Italy – than it was about incredible and iconic food and painting/photo ops.

St. John and Waters are well known in the South, but I doubt that "An Italian Palate" graces very many bookshelves where I live in the Finger Lakes region of Upstate New York. That didn't matter, though, because it was a very special gift for my wife and me.

OK, fast forward to a 2017 group trip that I had organized to Rome and Tuscany. One day we had a pasta-making lesson in a restaurant called *La Gramola* in the small, lovely little Tuscan town of Tavarnelle Val di Pesa (population of about 7,700) not far from Florence. Our group learned how to make ravioli and tagliatelle by hand in the morning, then took a short bus ride to another even smaller village, Tignano (pop. 250), for lunch and wine tasting. The itinerary called for returning to *La Gramola* that evening for a dinner made with some of the pasta we had helped create, and if *La Gramola* sounds familiar to some of you, it's because you read about it and its owners Massimo and Cecilia in an earlier chapter.

While waiting for that dinner, we had a couple hours to kill in Tavarnelle, which is not famous by any means but is picture-postcard pretty with cobblestone streets, off-the-beaten-path charm and many small shops with all sorts of artisan products. It is nestled in the Chianti hills almost exactly halfway between Florence and Siena, and its name comes from the word *taverna* – for tavern – because in the Middle Ages and the Renaissance it was a kind of resting point for travelers who were making the trip between the two famous cities.

Never mind all that history, though. While we had some free time, many of the ladies in our group filled it by making a beeline to those shops and contributing to the region's economy while another small group of us went off in search of a cold beer or Super Tuscan wine, another certain way to bolster that economy.

We came across a bar called *The Viola Club* on Via Roma, a main street in Tavarnelle. *Viola* is the Italian word for purple, which is the color of the uniforms worn by the most popular soccer team in that region, Florence. And indeed, inside the club that late afternoon, about two dozen men were clustered around a small TV watching a *Fiorentina* game. While the *tifosi* – or fans – cheered on their favorite soccer team inside, the American tourists sat outside, sipping our drinks and soaking up that famous Tuscan sun.

Paolo, the amicable owner of the club I would learn later, was our very attentive server, though he also was keeping close tabs on that game.

When it was time to leave, I went inside to settle up with Paolo, and – with the game over and Florence a winner – he had time to chat a bit more. He asked about our group, where we were from, where we were staying. I told him we were Americans staying in a villa near San Gimignano, and he invited us to come, as a group, to have dinner in the restaurant that was part of *The Viola Club*. In singing its praises, he made sure to tell me that his *mamma* was the cook, and what a great cook she was.

I told him we were on a tight schedule, but I would see what I could do about a possible dinner there some night. Then, to drive home his point about what a renowned restaurant it was, he took me back to his mother's kitchen to show me around. Back in *la cucina*, he also pulled out a book, and said, "An American writer even included *mamma* in his book."

You may be able to guess where this is going, though I still didn't have the slightest idea that the book he would pull out would be ... "An Italian Palate!!!"

There, on Page 81, was a photo of my new friend Paolo and his mother, Giuliana, with a small "Travel Journal" snippet about

223

St. John's visit to Tavarnelle Val di Pesa. There also is a recipe from Giuliana for *peposa*, which is basically Italian pot roast with a lot of pepper and garlic and cooked in – what else? – dry red wine, preferably Tuscan.

Needless to say, I was stunned when Paolo laid out that book and flipped to the photo of him and his mom. He was equally as stunned when I told him that I owned a copy of that very same book and it resided on my coffee table in my living room back in the United States. Of course, Paolo thought that perhaps the book was a bestseller in the States and that it probably graced many coffee tables, but I told him that was not the case.

"It's unbelievable to me, almost impossible to believe, really, that you would show me that book," I told him. It was a serendipitous moment to the highest degree and one that immediately bonded us as fast friends.

Giuliana had not yet arrived, but she would soon to prepare that evening's meals, and Paolo implored me to wait and meet her, but I just couldn't because I needed to catch up with the group at *La Gramola*. As we parted, I told him that if we couldn't bring the group back for dinner during this trip, I would at least keep in touch by email, which I have done, and then, *alla prossima* (remember your lessons from Chapter 30?), when I return to Tavarnelle Val di Pesa, I would stop in and meet *Mamma* the Chef.

When I caught up to the rest of the group, already sitting down for dinner in *La Gramola*, I must have had a look on my face like I'd seen a ghost. I still couldn't believe what had just happened at *The Viola Club*, and honestly, the more I repeated the story to my traveling companions, the more incredible it sounded to me.

That is not the end of this tale of super coincidences, either. It changes venues, though, by only about 4,000 miles, from Tuscany to Mississippi, which, a few months later, we visited with the friends who had gifted us "The Italian Palate." We were staying in Jackson, Mississippi and were headed to the historic Civil War battlefield of Vicksburg when our friends, the Barretts, mentioned that Wyatt Waters had a studio in the city of Clinton, which was on our route and would we like to pop in? Would we?

Clinton is a pretty college town, eerily similar to Tavarnelle Val di Pesa with its cobblestoned streets and bright, colorful homes. Waters' studio is about a 9-iron from the campus of Mississippi College in Clinton's downtown area, so we stopped in to see if he was around.

Unfortunately, he was not because he was packing and getting ready for another painting trip to – get this – Italy! The young lady who greeted us informed us of that before we started up a very pleasant, you're-not-from-around-here kind of conversation. We learned that she actually had spent some time in Upstate New York a few years back, and when we asked her where, we were floored when she said Mount Morris, a town that is about 55 miles west of where we live in Geneva. She said she had heard how beautiful Geneva was and had wanted to visit, but she was in our neck of the woods during a particularly difficult winter and was unable to make it to our city.

Still, we marveled at the "small-worldness" of the whole thing, just as I had marveled at my meeting with Paolo and "the book." We told her that story, and she loved it, promising that she would relate it to Wyatt next time she saw him. We then bought some prints and some other souvenirs, said our goodbyes, and headed off to Vicksburg to tour the famous battlefield.

I often recount how traveling in Italy never fails to disappoint and that it is magical, even – or maybe especially – when you're not looking for anything special. Now, I will forever add this tale to the list: When the pages of a coffee table book about traveling and cooking in Italy came to life in the quaint little Tuscan town of Tavarnelle Val di Pesa and led, down a swirling path, to a connection in Mississippi.

36

Making New 'Old' Friends in the Eternal City

Roma, Provincia di Roma, Lazio

Paese che vai, usanze che trovi. – *Traditional Italian proverb*
Literally: The country (or places) you visit, its customs you will find.
So: When in Rome, do as the Romans do.

Ok, so you're heading off to Rome, the extraordinary, celebrated, bustling Eternal City, and you're attempting to figure out some of the sights that you absolutely have got to check out on your visit, no ifs, ands or buts.

The Colosseum? Check.

The Roman Forum? Without a doubt.

The Spanish Steps and Trevi Fountain? Sure, they're very close to each other, so why not hit them both up?

St. Peter's, Vatican City and the Sistine Chapel? Absolutely.

The upper flat in the apartment building of Francesca Casalino's parents?

Uh ... excuse me. Come again?

You know, Francesca Casalino's parents' place. Apartment complex off Viale Lina Cavalieri. Outside the city center but still metropolitan Rome. North side, up near ... well, honestly, not really up near anything that anyone has ever heard of. A bend in the Tiber River is nearby, along with railroad tracks that originate in the famed Stazione Termini and a couple of parks. But there aren't any noted Roman ruins around there; no famous obelisks, cathedrals or chariot racing ovals. Nothing that Dan Brown has featured in any of his novels. Just apartment complexes, really; immense, people-packing apartment complexes. It's . where the middle-class Romans live when they can't afford – or don't want – to live in upscale neighborhoods like Trastevere or Testaccio.

It is exactly where 16 of us went for one memorable dinner party during a September 2017 trip to Rome and Tuscany. You won't find it in any guidebooks. You won't see travel guru Rick Steves talking about it on any of his shows. However, for our group, it turned out to be one of the most unforgettable experiences during a trip full of unforgettable experiences.

Francesca is part of a growing trend in travel – folks who open up their homes to strangers and prepare a typical meal of their city or region. It's sort of like the Airbnb movement where people do the same and offer travelers a room or two in their homes. In this case, however, it's dinner that is being provided.

I love authentic Italian restaurants, if you haven't been able to tell as you've made your way through these pages, but there is something even more special about sharing a typical meal with local folks in their home. I have had that experience dozens and dozens of times with *famiglia* and *amici* in the Old Country, but I was afraid that my American friends on this particular trip were not going to be able to feel those emotions as our group was slated to eat only in restaurants during the course of our trip. I wanted them to know what it was like to be welcomed into a typical home and to break bread and have a toast with real local folks.

I discovered Francesca on a website called "Like A Local," where she offered to prepare a magnificent, inexpensive – and typically Roman – home-cooked meal. The only issue was that Francesca was used to cooking for groups of four to six people, and here I was, looking for something for my wife and me and 14 of our closest friends to soak up that Roman experience. Francesca and I emailed back and forth, and eventually she said that while her own apartment in the historic center of Rome would be too small for such a robust dinner party, her parents had a larger flat, and they would be happy to accommodate us.

Initially, I told her that I could not possibly do that to her, or anyone's, parents – barge in with 16 loud American tourists. She insisted, however, that they would be pleased and honored to host us. I don't know exactly how she knew that, since we had never met, but eventually arrangements were made.

Francesca even lined up a driver with a 20-person van – Gianfranco, to be precise – who could take all 16 of us on the 45-minute ride from our hotel in the southwest corner of the metro area to her parents' flat. When I told her I also would love it if my friends could experience a real Roman neighborhood bar or tavern in an off-the-beaten-path part of the city, she arranged that, too, asking Gianfranco to drop us off at just such a joint for pre-dinner cocktails. And if you needed a sign that not many tourists ever rolled through that neighborhood, all you had to do was look at the faces of the handful of Roman barflies who were having some quiet drinks in that bar *before* the Americans, 16 strong, burst in. We were treated royally, however, and showed our appreciation to the bar staff by leaving something that is regarded as typically American: A nice-sized tip.

Another sign that this was not your normal sightseeing trip: Gianfranco, a native of Rome and a longtime limo and van driver, got more than a bit lost looking for the flat. It was not, he said, a part of Rome through which he regularly was asked to navigate. Understood, I said, all part of the *avventura* – our adventure.

Romans – and many Italians, actually – are celebrated for being fashionably late. So we, after a Happy Hour stop at the neighborhood joint and Gianfranco's sketchy knowledge of the area, arrived at Francesca's parents' apartment complex about half an hour tardy for a typically-late 8:30 p.m. Roman dinner. Gianfranco, even after he pulled his vehicle to a stop in the complex, was unable to tell which of the buildings was that of Francesca's parents, so he phoned them and asked them to offer us a signal. Easy enough, they said. They would be flashing the lights on their outdoor patio as a welcoming sign. It didn't take us long to notice the *benvenuti* strobe off in the distance, and we made our joyous way to our hosts' apartment.

After animated hellos and introductions – no doubt influenced on our part by the local cocktails – the early going was, I must say, a tiny bit subdued. Everyone, on both sides of the dinner party, was a tad reserved, as if we all were feeling each other out. In the back of my mind, though, I still couldn't believe these lovely Roman folks had agreed to have their lives thrown into a tizzy by hosting this group of *stranieri*, or strangers. Plus, did I mention it was Sept. 11? And the Americans had to begin the evening with a commemorative, somber moment of silence? We did, and our new international *amici* joined us in a heartfelt scene of international kinship that would have melted your heart if you'd been there.

That was, of course, only the beginning. It would be the last time any of us were quiet all night.

Mom and Dad – who would be Tina and Beppe as we were very happy to learn – were both recently retired from state jobs, she in a municipal office, he with the railroad. They knew that Francesca put on these dinners for absolute strangers, but they admitted that they weren't particularly keen on the idea, not knowing who might walk through their only daughter's door demanding a home-cooked meal.

However, by the end of the evening? After a Prosecco toast and more than a few bottles of local wines; after some of the best lasagna we've ever had, "light but rich," as we jokingly called it with homemade noodles as thin as a page of the morning newspaper; after chicken cacciatore in a white wine sauce with anchovies, garlic and capers; after an antipasto platter that included amazing olives, mortadella panini, fresh ricotta and robiola cheese; after exquisite tiramisu for dessert, served elegantly in china tea cups; after espresso, grappa and limoncello? By the end of the evening, we were old, familiar, dear and fast friends. Oh, and we were stuffed.

Francesca spoke English very well, but Tina and Beppe did not. Didn't matter. Stories about all our families flew in all directions. My friends only spoke a smattering of Italian. Again, it didn't matter. We told each other about our kids, our jobs, our lives. In between courses, a few of our folks would go out on the balcony for fresh air; Tina or Beppe, and sometimes both, would join them to tell stories, as best as the language differences would allow. Others would lean back in their chairs at the table, and Francesca would engage them in tales about what it is like to live in the Eternal City. As the next course would be placed reverently on the table, everyone would reassemble from their various spots, utensils in hand, ready to dive into the next dish of Roman exquisiteness.

This played out for all the courses.

For the dessert course – that heavenly tiramisu – the wait seemed to be exceptionally long, however. It was gaining on midnight, and I was getting worried that we were keeping these generous folks up way too late. In addition, we had an early-morning engagement the next day at the Vatican. I went into the kitchen to see what the delay might be, and I found Francesca, Tina and Beppe relaxing, having coffee, laughing and chatting. They did not want to "rush" their guests out the door, they said, so they were taking their time getting the dessert and coffee prepared. So, it was me – telling them that we already had intruded way too much on their time – practically begging and "rushing" them to serve the final course.

It was well past midnight when we finally left our new, old friends, and they told us, "Don't you ever come to Rome again without coming to visit us." In fact, Beppe told me something similar to what Liberio Profeta from Sicily told me back in Chapter 31 – that I was no longer allowed to stay in hotels in Rome, that whenever I visit the Eternal City in the future, I have a place to stay: their flat; eternally.

Francesca texted me the next day to say that now – finally – her parents understood why she did these meals. She said that they told her, "If everyone you host is like that group, we want to help you all the time!"

It made me proud that we had been such good ambassadors for America, and that we had found such a beautiful Roman family with which to share a memorable evening in Roma.

Imagine my surprise, too, when I found out a few months later that Francesca was even more famous than I had imagined – or at least was becoming famous. A website called "smart magazine," which endeavors to discover solutions for today's urban challenges, sent its British film crew, Topjaw, to Rome to discover a foreign culture in a series called Challenge Accepted. You can find the 5½-minute clip on YouTube. Jesse, the lead man of the crew, enlists a local Roman to show him some of the city's hot spots and to teach him how to cook traditional Roman meals. The person he selected to help him learn all things Roman was none other than our friend Francesca – he found her, he says, due to "rave reviews" that she received online, hopefully mine included.

The neat thing is that as the segment draws to a close, Jesse is going to prepare a meal for Francesca's parents using the tips he learned from her. And then, there they are on the video – our other new friends Beppe and Tina! – enjoying Jesse's dinner, which included, by the way, that luscious tiramisu for dessert.

I will never say to anyone planning a visit to the Eternal City, forget the Colosseum … or the Vatican … or the Spanish Steps. But here's the deal: If you're ever in Rome, look up Francesca Casalino and her family. You'll be richly rewarded for doing so.

37

Il Paradiso di Frassina - Of Grapevines and Mozart

Montalcino, Provincia di Siena, Toscana

Cambiano i suonatori ma la musica è sempre quella. – *Old Italian proverb*
Literally: The musicians change, but the music remains the same.
Translation: The song remains the same.

La vera musica, che sa far ridere e all'improvviso ti aiuta a piangere. –
Paolo Conte, singer, composer, pianist
Translation: Real music makes you laugh and then suddenly helps
you cry.

It was like a scene from a movie. Or a dream.

Out group – about twenty of us – was enjoying almost shockingly
blue skies, with a couple of wispy white clouds dancing through every
now and then. We were sitting under large white lawn umbrellas at tables dressed in bright red tablecloths.

The grass and fields were the lush definition of green that only
idyllic conditions can produce. Off in the distance, a herd of grazing
white sheep broke up all that green.

It was mid-May, so the grapevines that covered much of the rolling landscape also were primarily green, having already flowered. But at
the end of each row of vines, bushes of bright red or pink roses added
splashes of colors that looked like an artist had simply taken a brush and
dribbled in some color to accent the green. We learned later that those
vibrant flowers also played a role in the vineyard environment – if the

plants are attacked by bacteria or diseases such as black rot or mildew, it is expected that the flowers will be afflicted with any malady first, thus hopefully sparing the grapes.

To top off this incredible scene that was straight out of "The Great Gatsby" or something, we were being soothed by the melodic and relaxing strains of classical music playing not only all around us but also being piped straight down to those vines via very modern means – Bose all-weather speakers. Mozart, Chopin, Beethoven. The music was all part of the plan for winery owner Giancarlo Cignozzi who had the brilliant thought that, "Hey, if music is good for house plants, why wouldn't it make my grapes grow sweeter and healthier?" He started by playing the accordion – yes, Dad's favorite *cor-DEEN* – directly to his grapes, and by the time of our visit had expanded to wiring those speakers throughout the entire vineyard.

We were at *Il Paradiso di Frassina*, just outside the medieval Tuscan wine town of Montalcino, in the spring of 2005. With the violins and cellos serenading us, and the sun shining brightly, and the ruby red Super Tuscan Brunello di Montalcino being poured generously by our host, Giancarlo's wife Diana Grandi, we indeed felt like we were in paradise.

The colors vibrant. The air sweet. The wine exquisitely smooth. The music relaxing. It was, as I said, like a scene from a movie. We expected Roberto Benigni to come bouncing around the corner. Or Sophia Loren.

Even our bus driver Salvatore was joining us, which is something bus drivers on these group excursions rarely do. But my Dad was with us on this trip and had become fast friends with the young driver, so when he put his arm around him and invited him to sit and lounge with us on the second to last day of our trip, Salvatore took him up on it. Thus, the "family" was complete.

The folks at *Il Paradiso di Frassina* were kicking things up a notch with their hospitality, but the setting was one of those typically beautiful scenes that many have experienced while visiting Italy's most famous region, Tuscany. Everywhere you look there is beauty, both in its landscapes and its people. We all have snapshots in our mind of how we hope things are going to look once we get there, and so often the real settings don't live up to those fantasies. Not so, *la bella Toscana*. Every time I have visited, the real photos that I bring home with me and fill my albums or iPads with are even better than those snapshots I had imagined beforehand.

OK, back to *Il Paradiso di Frassina*, which is headquartered in a renovated 1,000-year-old farmstead at the foot of the Montosoli hill outside of Montalcino, a town of about 6,000 people that was renowned during the Middle Ages for its shoes and leather goods; now it is celebrated primarily for its luscious Brunello wine, which would always show up in any discussion of Italy's best reds. After a tour of the winery, which was under the microscope at the time by researchers at both the University of Florence and the University of Pisa who were studying the effects of Mozart on the grapes, we knew we were going to be treated to a wine-and-cheese tasting.

However, it was much more than that. Rather than a wine "tasting," it was a wine "drinking," with as much of the Brunello, which goes for $40-50 a bottle, as we wanted. And the food to go with it, set out buffet style, under those white lawn umbrellas, was much more than just slices of the local homemade pecorino cheese. It was typical Tuscan fare, including fresh salamis and prosciutto and highlighted by bowls of *ribollita*, the region's famous bread-and-vegetable soup that includes black-leaf kale, cabbage, Swiss chard, beans and many other vegetables, including carrots, onions and celery. The thick soup has two distinct characteristics, at least on this bucolic day: No. 1) it practically cries out to be scooped up on a slice of crusty Tuscan bread, an action that is called *fare la scarpetta* in Italian, or "make like a little shoe" to mop up all the goodness, and No. 2) it begs to be washed down with another sip of Brunello.

To top off this memorable afternoon, which still seems surreal even as I think back on it over a decade later, Diana and Giancarlo's pretty little five-year-old daughter, Gea – for whom one of their wines was named – serenaded us with traditional Italian folksongs.

Salvatore (left), who drove the coach to Montalcino, became part of our "family" – dubbed "cousin" Salvatore by my father.

Oh, and did I mention that classical music was playing all around us, too? It was a jubilee for all the senses, a real slice of Tuscan life that can't truly be captured by printed words on a page. It definitely was something that we all will remember for the rest of our lives and will always have us longing to return to *la bella Toscana*.

Back to the musical study in this small vineyard. Cignozzi's experiment was based on the fact that music is known to improve the quality of life of humans and animals, so why not plants, he thought, especially the Sangiovese grapes that are the primary varietal in Brunello? Once he started pumping music to the vines, he says he observed much hardier, much healthier and more disease resistant grapes that he also felt ripened much more consistently and grew larger toward the source of the sound.

The scientific world, of course, does not rely on such anecdotal stories from quaint winemakers, hence the call to arms – and laptops

– by researchers in Florence and Pisa. Their results were detailed in a 2016 piece on CBS News.

Reporter Seth Doane first asked Giancarlo and his son, Ulisse, what they thought about the section of their vineyards where the grapes were serenaded all day, every day, and they told him those plants were more robust. They added that those closest to the speakers had higher sugar content.

Uh huh, sure they did.

So, Doane went to Stefano Mancuso, a plant scientist at the University of Florence, and asked him, "When you first heard about this guy growing grapes and playing music, what did you think?"

"That he was another ... another crazy guy," the professor said.

"These vines like Mozart?" Doane asked.

"It's very difficult to say that plants like classical music – Wagner, Mozart, or whatever you want. What they are able actually to do is to perceive sounds and specific frequencies," Mancuso explained scientifically, saying they might actually be bolstered by almost any kind of music or sound.

A side benefit, he noted, was that the music seemed to keep harmful insects at bay, making them unable to breed, so the vineyard doesn't have to use any pesticides. The music also seems to scare away birds and other creatures that normally would eat the grapes.

Giancarlo took all the empirical data and information into account – the stuff about frequencies and perceptions of sounds – and said to Doane, simply, "I prefer the music. Sorry, but I'm very romantic!"

So, there we are then, an Italian winemaker talking about romance, lovely strains of classical music being played all around, amazing food and famous wine, an enchanting old farmhouse, alluring scenery, a gathering of smiling friends.

This seems like as good a place as any to end not only this section on exploring Italy but this book, in general – this collection of tales that began with my Italian and Italian-American family and wound its way through our life from George Washing Machine to soccer to choir practice and ended with neat travels in the Old Country.

I hope you took the hint offered in the beginning and plopped a peach slice or two into your wine as you ambled through the pages. I hope the stories reminded you of your own family in one way or another, and I hope they encouraged you to find out for yourself what Italy is all about and make a trip across the Atlantic to visit.

My 21st trip was in September in 2018 for my Zio Enzo's funeral, and as I write this book, I am looking forward to my 22nd trip, which will be in September of 2019, another of those group trips, this time to the Amalfi Coast and to the Adriatic Coast.

Visiting the land that is very much a part of my makeup has made me learn to appreciate America even more. As even Dad would say, America is No. 1 for sure … and Italy is a close No. 2.

That leads me to another of those timeworn Italian proverbs that have been sprinkled throughout these pages and that say so much in just a few words: *A ogni uccello il suo nido è bello.*

In English: Every bird finds his own nest beautiful, the Italian equivalent of our "home sweet home."

It's my sincerest hope that we have become close friends – *amici* or *paisani* – as we have traveled through these pages together, and so I will leave you with just one more of those incredible traditional proverbs:

Amici e vini sono meglio vecchi.

Friends and wine are best aged.

REVIEWS

Reading Mike Cutillo's *George Washing Machine* is like breathing a refreshing mix of clean Mediterranean and upstate New York air. The book is part history, part travelogue and above all a personal journal wrapped in a witty, clever writing style that showcases the author's years as a journalist and keen observer of people and family. Especially his father. While this is Cutillo's first book – after decades of producing many thousands of column inches of newspaper columns, news & sports stories and editorials – expect readers to be asking for more. And soon.

— Michael J. Fitzgerald
Author of The Devil's Pipeline *and other novels.*

Mike Cutillo gives us a rollicking read with this collection of gentle vignettes and reflections on immigrant life and culture in America over the last sixty-five years. Although his gently whimsical stories explore the lives of Italian-Americans in particular, they also illuminate the richness more broadly of U.S. immigrant life and culture. This page-turner kept me engaged and laughing. I highly recommend it for anyone with an interest in immigrant family life, values, and customs. *George Washing Machine* is a significant contribution to U.S. immigration literature.

— Robert E. May
Professor emeritus of history at Purdue University
and author of numerous books, including his most recent,
"Yuletide in Dixie," due out in October 2019.

George Washing Machine recounts how the Cutillo family successfully juggles enjoying life in America while steadfastly clinging to its Italian heritage. A first generation Italian-American, Mike Cutillo, using his immigrant father as a focal point and supported by numerous return visits to Italy, relates the transition from being Italian to Italian-American. A great family memoir, this book should also appeal to others interested in Italian culture.

— *Donald F. Staffo*
Long-time, educator, author and
a proud Italian-American

As I read Mike's lively *stufato (stew)*, I marveled at the timing of this rich and lovely story: The way Mike's father, Michele, and other immigrants have helped form the backbone of our country is among the things that give us so much to celebrate. Utilizing the keen eyes and deep insights of the award-winning journalist he is, Mike deftly weaves together the saga of his father's life in two worlds. If you wonder at all about America's story, this is it. Get ready to laugh and cry and fall in love with Michele Cutillo. As for his son, Mike, well, all he does is collect stories … and write them like a song.

— *John Erardi*
Author of "Tony Perez: From Cuba to Cooperstown,"
National Baseball Hall of Fame voter and Syracuse native

ACKNOWLEDGMENTS

So many people say, "You know, I ought to write a book ..."

I was one of them. I kept saying it ... and saying it ... and saying it. All talk, no action.

Two of my high school buddies, Ken Boyd and Kevin Hulslander – both of whom I'm proud to say have turned into lifetime pals, who knew that way back then? – always told me that they were sure I would. I would just nod.

My daughter, Kristine – one of the most creative people I know who also happens to have the gentlest and purest of souls – was absolutely, positively sure that I would. Some day. I wasn't so sure, yet here we are. She knows her old man better than her old man knows himself.

My sisters, all younger, all targets of my childhood pranks and needling – Teresa, Lisa and Jennifer – they never really said it, but I know they hoped it. They knew I was the keeper of the records, the sponge who soaked up all Dad's stories, the family tree creator, the chronicler. They didn't say, "Write a book," so much as when I finally started to, they let out a deep breath, almost collectively, and said, "Geez, it's about time." Their turn to needle me.

My Mom, Sylvia, who died in 2008 – occasional Strega drinker, lover of jigsaw puzzles, Scrabble, crosswords, and the most voracious reader I ever knew; check that, Mom didn't read a book so much as she absorbed it. Forced to grow up at a too-young age when her father died and she was charged with watching her younger siblings, she is watching over all of us now. I would say, "Mom, I'm going to write a book someday," and no matter how many times I said it ... over and over ... all talk, no action, she would say, "There's no doubt about that, honey."

My longtime colleague, right-hand man and golf partner – not necessarily in that order – Alan Brignall, and my former boss-turned-into-great friend Paul Barrett, one of the finest publishers of small-town newspapers in America and a better storyteller than me with his Southern upbringing, when I told them I was writing a book, they both said, "Of course you are."

My wife, Jan, beautiful inside and out, passionate, fun-loving, with a heart as big as the Atlantic Ocean, knew that a lifelong dream of mine was to write a book, and when I finally got around to working on this project, she looked at me with her pretty big eyes and said, "There you go, your dream is coming true." I love you.

You all have inspired me, encouraged me, cheered for me and most of all, loved me.

There are so many others to mention that I could write a separate book on that alone, but to acknowledge a few that need to be: My mother-in-law Josie and father-in-law John Gawlik, who don't care what I write but love every word; my seventh-grade English teacher Tom McKee, who hatched the idea within me to become a sportswriter; Norm Jollow, late *Finger Lakes Times* sports editor who gave me my first full-time newspaper job; my great friends – and incredibly talented authors – Michael Fitzgerald, John Erardi, Bob May, and Don Staffo – thank you for your testimonials, if my book is half as good as yours, I'll be blessed; Sal Moschella, retired editor of the "Golden Lion" newsletter for the New York State Sons and Daughters of Italy in America, who encouraged me to tell my Italian-American stories for OSDIA members; and all my friends and relatives here in America and in Italy, thank you for everything.

A special thank you also to my editor on this project, Tiziano Thomas Dossena of Idea Press. Never having been through this process before, I had enough questions for him to fill up a 55-gallon wine barrel. Tiziano very graciously and professionally answered every single one of them, and when I thought up even more, he said, very kindly, "Listen, not only will I be your editor on this project, but I will be your friend," and that is, indeed, what he has proven to be.

While we were working on this book together, I was thrilled to learn that – on June 1, 2019, in front of statewide delegates and dignitaries – Tiziano was presented the prestigious 2019 OSDIA Literary Award, presented by New York State Comptroller Thomas DiNapoli. It was presented to him "for his contribution to the Italian American Experience in America." I could not be prouder of my editor … and my friend.

And finally, a few words – OK, a few *more* words – about the indisputable, unmistakable star of this book, the man who brought us George Washing Machine, portables and submarine races, my Dad, Michele.

Dad, without you, I would not only not be a "son" of Italy, but I would not be half the man that I am today. You gave us everything that you had; every single thing that you did was for your family and friends. You taught us to love and to respect, to work hard and even to play hard. You showed us not only your love for your own culture and heritage but also how very much you love the United States of America. There are dozens of people – maybe hundreds – who would look at you and say that you are their best friend or among their best friends. That is special. You are special.

When I told you that I was writing a book and that it was mostly going to be about you and your stories, you said, "Why would you want to write about me?"

I think this book answers that question. *Ti voglio tanto bene, papà. Grazie di tutto.*

ABOUT THE AUTHOR

Born in Syracuse, New York, Mike Cutillo grew up in Baldwinsville, graduated from C.W. Baker High School in 1978 and Magna Cum laude from St. John Fisher College (Rochester) in 1982 with a BA in Communications/Journalism and minors in Business Management and Italian.

He has been a journalist, a reporter and an editor in Upstate New York since 1982, primarily in the Finger Lakes region where he has worked for the daily *Finger Lakes Times* (Geneva) for over 30 years as a sports writer, sports editor and news editor and has been the executive editor since 2011. He also has been a regional reporter for the *Rochester Democrat & Chronicle* and a sports editor for the *Canandaigua Daily Messenger.*

George Washing Machine is his first book, but he has won numerous writing awards from the New York State Associated Press, the New York and Pennsylvania Publishers Associations and GateHouse Media. He also has had articles published in *Mountain Home* and *College Sports* magazines and has been a regular columnist for over 20 years for the *Golden Lion*, the official publication of the Grand Lodge of New York Order Sons and Daughters of Italy in America.

He has traveled to Italy over 20 times and between 2001 and 2019 he has organized nine group trips through his local Geneva Sons of Italy lodge, escorting over 400 people to various parts of Italy, including Tuscany, Venice, the Lakes Region, the Amalfi and Adriatic coasts, Rome, Calabria and Sicily.

Cutillo lives in Geneva with his wife, Jan. He has a grown daughter, Kristine, who lives in North Carolina.

Made in the USA
Lexington, KY
15 December 2019